I0161490

EVOLUTION
OF A BROKEN
HEART

GP

GODZCHILD PUBLICATIONS

Copyright © 2017 by Valerio Henriquez

Published by Godzchild Publications
a division of Godzchild, Inc.
22 Halleck St., Newark, NJ 07104
www.godzchildproductions.net

Printed in the United States of America 2017 - 1st Edition
Cover art by Frank Martinez Andujar, Arecibo PR.
Graphics by Joanna Harris, Memphis TN.

All rights reserved. Except as permitted under the U.S. Copyright Act of 1976, this publication shall not be broadcast, rewritten, distributed, or transmitted, electronically or copied, in any form, or stored in a database or retrieval system, without prior written permission from the author.

Library of Congress Cataloging-in-Publications Data
Evolution of a Broken Heart/Valerio Henriquez

ISBN   978-1-942705-44-4 (pbk.)
        978-1-942705-45-1 (ePub)

1. Henriquez, Valerio 2. Destiny 3. Purpose 4. Self-Help 5. Poetry
6. Divorce 7. Christianity 8. Relgious 9. Spirituality 10. Discovery

Unless otherwise identified, all Scripture quotations in this publication are taken from the The King James Version (KJV). All rights reserved.

2017

All of the contents within this book are the sole copyrighted property of Valerio Henriquez 3rd. The use and reproduction of this content without the author's written permission is strictly unauthorized. Some names and identifying details have been changed to protect the privacy of individuals.

This book is dedicated to my loving God "The Great I am", and His son Jesus Christ, who paid for my sins and rid me of my guilt. His words (Deut 31:6, "He will never leave you nor forsake you") held fast in my heart during the darkest hours of my lost life. And Jesus' love, guided me through the desert, towards an oasis of blessings, and inspired me to write this book, so that others who are going through the same journey would know that they are not alone.
I am forever grateful.

TABLE OF CONTENTS

When I started this journey my heart was anorexic and starved. Feeding off of itself, chained up to a fence post with no food nor water.

Neglected and sometimes kicked by that person that was supposed to take care of it.

Sometimes people wonder:
What is the mystique behind that story or poem?
Why did that person write that?
What caused him or her to feel that way?
What was the inspiration behind it?

So along with my poems and short stories, I'm giving you my personal journal of my journey during the past few years, as well as a lot of the reasons why I wrote what I did.

In this Journal of poetry, the chapters are broken up like this:
The first one, named Caído (which means fallen in Spanish) is the affair I had with a beautiful women, and my walk away from God.

The second Chapter "Corazones roto se ropen" (Translated: Broken hearts get broken) is the break up between myself and my affair partner.

The third is about the deep hole of depression I fell into, and was given hope by another beautiful lady that stepped into my life and became my guiding light out of the deep dark hole. Hence the title: "Luz de mi Corazon" (Heart light).

In the fourth, "Incipere" (Latin for inspire) I document the breakup and the inspirational healing and movement to become whole again. That's why the chapters from this one forward are in Latin. Thus the translations seem to seep in better to personify the Lords touch in my life.

The fifth, "Illustratum" (Latin for Light) was my coming home to God. Finding him as my source of light, and no longer depending on the human aspect to be healed, but depending and relying on his words to be whole again.

The sixth, "Sanitatum (Healing) is the renewing process of healing we all continue to go through. The movement forward in life, daring to live, inspired by God, walking the path he set before me. It's the inspiration to live life purposely, as God deemed us to do. My renewed "Faith Walk".

They say that two wrongs don't make a right.

But I beg to differ on that, and wish to rephrase it, when it comes to relationships. One right and one wrong does not make a right. You both have to be positive, and "right" with all decisions (even though you might not like it) in order for a marriage or relationship to work. The reason is, one person doing all the work just frustrates that person doing the work, and aggravates the person not doing anything to better the relationship (in some instances, like mine, it's because they're in denial).

The twenty nine and a half year old marriage I had, had an expiration date that far outlived itself. It was time to move on to new seasons and chapters in both of our lives (hers and mine).

Like an ink blot or random cloud in the sky, when people looked at our marriage it became whatever cool illusion anyone wanted to see.

I wrote this book because there's a lot of misconception out there about people who have cheated on their spouses. Pointing fingers will always favor the "loud victim" and never notice the quiet reason as to why someone, who is a pillar of a community, a great dad/mom, an all around decent person, in his/her right mind would get divorced after being married so long.

As you read this book mark it up. Put notes about your thoughts and experience on how you relate to certain topics. And highlight your favorite parts and read them over and over again, especially when you're down to remind you that you're not alone. Make this book and its poems your own. Read them again slowly capturing the images they place in your mind.

Everyone has a dark chapter in their life they don't want to be read out loud.
Here is mine.

In poetry and journal form.

CHAPTER 1

Caído (Fallen)

A BAD BEGINNING

It was a bad thing from the get go.

The marriage was a sham.

The term "fake it till you make it" was what I was trying to live by.

I figured if I worked hard enough, earned enough money, gave her nice gifts (Mercedes Benz, diamond rings, mink coat) then spend time with her watching her movies on the couch (oh how I hate Downton Abbey), took her out to eat, made more money and became the best father and husband that I could become, that it would compensate for this loveless, lackluster, emotionless, marriage we had.

Maybe we could do like the old-timers before us, who got together and learned to love each other.

No. Not us.

As time went on and it became more and more miserable, I became more and more desperate to make it work out.

I read books, went to seminars, associated with happy couples, picked their minds and tried to do whatever I could to improve myself and our relationship. And not to her fault, she did too!

She attended ladies seminars and meetings with me.

And she took some really great notes!

Afterwards we would bounce the ideas off of each other of what we would do and needed to do to be happy and successful together as a couple and a family.

Then within a week or two, the idea would peter out, and we were back to the same routine. Fighting (over sex, money, how to bring up kids, chores), saying negative comments and "digs" to each other, and so on. When we fought the kids would leave the house or lock themselves in their rooms. Sometimes they would tell me, "Dad! Stop it. You know how she is, dad. Just let it go so she can stop". So I did.

My ex-wife and I met via her sister, who I worked with. And after dating a few months, I had gotten her pregnant. When she told me the news, she said that she didn't need a man to raise her child, and that she would probably move into the projects and get on welfare to support herself and the baby. I freaked and said "No way! My kid is not growing up in the projects (of New York)". So I asked her to marry me and come live with me in my parent's basement, while I attended St. John's University so that I may be accepted into law school, to become a Contract lawyer.

And she did. After two years of living in my parents' basement, she became tired of it and started telling me how miserable she was. She wanted out of the basement, and especially away from my mother. I asked and begged her to hold on and wait until I finished law school (I was 21 at the time), and then we could move anywhere in New York that she wanted to live. But she kept threatening to leave with my daughter and move into the projects. So I did the next best thing, I joined the Navy (Submarine Force). After various schools I finally moved her (via the Navy) to San Diego California, where we had an apartment the size of a hotel room for six hundred dollars a month (which at that time (1986), as an E2, was half my pay). We were extremely poor, but lived together. She was a few months pregnant with my son at the time of the move, and a few month later we had a baby boy.

From San Diego, the Navy then moved us to my permanent duty station in Charleston, South Carolina. After a few months in an apartment we found a nice neighborhood next to the Submarine base in Goose Creek, and bought a small house on Oak Grove Road. During our stay in Goose Creek, I would go out to sea for months at a time, and when I'd get back, she would ask me when I was going out to sea again and she would have the kids chime in, "Dad when are you leaving again? We want you to leave." With my family turned against me, I figured that I needed to get out of the Navy, so that I can save my family and be the dad that I was supposed to be. Let me tell you that I loved the Naval Submarine life. If you would ask me now if I'd like to do a sea tour again, I would in a heartbeat. But I wanted to leave to become the dad I wasn't allowed to be while out at sea. So after back to back sea tours (what we call, sarcastically a "Navy good deal"), it was time for me to head to shore duty in Memphis Tennessee, at the Millington Naval Air Station.

Now that I was home on a daily basis in Memphis, things turned for us. I had gotten out of the Navy and pursued various jobs with startup companies during the Internet boom. We started to argue more often and at various times she threatened to leave me, and take the kids to live in Brooklyn, New York with her family. It got to the point that one time, while arguing over dirty dishes in the sink, she broke the dishes on the floor, grabbed the corner of our Bassett china cabinet and tried to push it off of the wall on top of me, while the kids screamed and cried. I was lucky enough to push it back up, and grab her and hold her while she hit me and screamed at me how much she hated me. I couldn't believe that dirty dishes had set her off, and after that episode, I did my best to clear the sink and take care of any other idiosyncrasies before she came home, to avoid any conflict. That didn't work either.

As time gave in, life became more and more difficult for us. The marriage wasn't getting any better. In my mind's eye I had a vision of me and my bride retiring young, early in life, walking the beaches of the world, observing sunsets and sunrises together, but it wasn't going to happen. Not with us.

We didn't have that chemistry nor that polarity that brings couples together.

We attended church, looked really good and polished on the outside. In front of people we behaved and lifted each other up (the opposite of what was happening behind closed doors). We seemed like the perfect couple that was united in all aspects of life raising awesome kids.

Then I came to the realization that that's all it was. A vision. An optical illusion in my mind, that wasn't going to happen. It was a sham and I was fooling myself. The different comments and jabs she kept saying over and over again echoed in my mind continuously. "I really only love you like a brother". "If you want sex, do me a favor and go find yourself a girlfriend!" "Leave me the f**k alone ", "I'm leaving you, I want to be by myself! I f**king hate you!" You'd think that I'd get a clue? No not me, Mr. Fixit.

My head and heart were in despair. I'd get migraines that would last for days. Sometime the migraines were so bad that they would disable me. I'd come home from work, take pills and lie in bed with the pillow over my head in total darkness and silence. I was broken, and there was no resolve to fix me. I didn't know why or how I could fix this anymore. I was beside myself, wanting to die, because I had failed continuously. And every attempt to fix this marriage failed dramatically.

They say when you're happy, you hear the music and rejoice. But when you're sad you hear the lyrics and understand. During this time I related a lot to a music band called Lincoln Park. Especially to a song called Numb. That was basically the song of my existence, with the chorus continuously echoing in my mind.

When a guy is that down in desperation and depression, with no relief or help in site, and he hears the comments that she kept drilling in my mind for over twenty years, he starts thinking about the options proposed to him by the person saying them.

I had placed both of our older kids through private school, and we were raising my wife's niece. I had her enrolled in private school and she had made some girlfriends. I was the dad that always took her and picked her up from school, and to her medical appointment after school, and even to play time with her friends. One day while in the car line picking her up from school, I saw this red convertible with this knock out red headed women behind the driver's seat. I'll always remember that day clearly. It was sunny and hot, the school year had started, she had the top down on her convertible, and a slight breeze brushed her long straight red hair back. She had her giant sun glasses up on her head, and took them off, brushed her long hair back with her fingers and placed the glasses on her face again. Then the car line moved on and I didn't see her again.

One day when I picked the youngest up from private school, she had told me about this new girl she had met in class and she wanted to go over her house to play. So, being the kid taxi driver dad that I was, I said sure, and I was delighted to do so for various reasons. One, it got me out of the house, and two, it beat having her hanging around the house and hearing me and my spouse fight. So I called the kids mom and set the date to take my kid over and drop her off to play with hers at their house.

As I pulled into the driveway of my niece's new play friend's house, there was a red convertible sitting in the garage. When I entered the house to meet the parents, she appeared. The Redhead from the car line. I was awe struck that I had finally gotten to meet her. Her husband was present and he didn't think anything about me being there. The girls met and ran upstairs, while the husband played x-box in the living room, adjacent to the kitchen where the Redhead and I stood and talked. After a few play dates the girls became best friends and started playing regularly at each other's house. When I'd drop her off, her mom would invite me in and I'd stop and visit for a while, and when she brought her daughter over, she'd hang and visit for a few minutes as well. I though nothing about it, except that I got the privilege to speak to an intelligent beautiful women who was positive, upbeat, always smiling, happy and had the same likes and point of view on life as I did. As time went on we had built a friendship, and she started telling me how awesome of a parent I was and how I was the manliest guy she's ever met. She'd always lift me up when she saw me, and would start complementing me on everything I did. We both liked flowers and she appreciated my care and design of my flower beds. At one point, during a visit with her husband at our house, my wife (at the time) even suggested that she help me with the flower beds, because she hated dealing with me and the stupid flowers. It actually got to the point that the Redhead and I would converse every other day about the kids and stuff in general. I'd be conversing with her on the phone and her husband would say, who is that on the phone, and she would reply "It's Valerio". And he say, "OK". He had no clue nor did he care who she was talking to, as long as she left him alone to play his x-box. Yes, she was an x-box widow. Totally ignored. My wife and her husband even called us BFF's. He'd tell her to leave him alone and call me about stuff, and my wife would tell me to call her, my BFF about things. It was crazy. They would pawn us off to each other!

At times my wife would even inject comments during our fights about (her) my BFF. Like "why don't you go and hang out with your

BFF…..call your BFF…tell your BFF…so what did your BFF say? …what did you tell your BFF?"

At first we had innocent conversations and spoke of things we had in common, like kids, flowers, movies, medicine, books, cars, finances, spouses, and clothes. And then it got flirtatious, and the obvious happened. We had an affair.

It went against the grain of all of my beliefs and being. You see my step father (Jose) had always cheated on my step mom (who was my aunt: Naty) and he would come home drunk with lipstick on his shirt and start a fight with her.

One day as a fight was brewing (in my childhood household) and Jose was about to hit Naty and I grabbed him and threw him on the floor (as a young 14 year old boy).

I then revved up my fist up to knock him out and he looked at me and stated to cry. I stopped in mid punch. And he said "go ahead, do it, I deserve it! I'm no good!"

At that point I had gotten off of him and told him, "No! I'm not going to hit you, nor am I ever going to be like you". And that pain resonated with me forever, because as a kid, it really hurt to see my mother (Naty) cry and break down because of step father's (Jose) drunken reckless behavior. And as a kid it caused me a lot of pain and suffering. So when all of these feeling for this Redhead started to muster up, all I can see and feel was that little boy, in total pain, telling his step dad that he wasn't going to be like him. And here I was heading down the same path, inch by inch, step by step, word by word, thought by thought. There were times that I cried on my knees, and swore to God to deliver me from these thoughts and this passion I was feeling for this woman. But I kept failing and falling over and over again on the sword of my thoughts, to the point where I started writing poetry about it, as a release from the guilt, to justify why I was doing what I was doing (The Affair).

And after the first intimate encounter with the Redhead, I knew that my marriage was over.

I knew that I wasn't a crappy husband and that I could do better. I should do better and she (my ex-wife) could do better than me too! There was someone out there for her, and it wasn't me.

We were clinging on to our misery because we had become co-dependent on each other.

And it was time to stop this train wreck.

Someone had to pull the bandage. And it had to be me.

You see, before the affair I was at a point in my life where I didn't give a s**t anymore. I bought a Harley Davidson, Road Glide Ultra, and I acted extremely crazy with it. I'd get up at 5 AM to go to work blasting Linkin Park on the Radio, and what was supposed to be a 30-40 minute ride to work, happened in less than 15 minutes. I'd push that 800 pound beast at over 100 mph on the highway and through the streets of south Memphis praying for a truck or something to come out and take me out.

I was even thinking of saying "f**k it all" to my life, family, job, house, church, cars and everything I had. I was just going to take my bike and join a local outlaw motor cycle club, and hang out with the guys, and become one of them. They'd be my brothers and they would understand me best, just like when I was on Submarines. I wanted a brotherhood that I could relate to and get away from my misery.

I was at the lowest of lows in my life and I went to seek help.

First I went to a Christian Psychologist. The same guy that was treating our youngest daughter. This doctor had tested her and diagnosed her with ADHD, Asperger's and a few other things. I spoke to this doctor about my depression, and how lousy my marriage was, how my wife was always threatening to leave me, and how we were constantly in a battle fighting and picking on each other.

His solution, since he was treating our daughter at the same time (who supposedly had all the issues), was to get rid of her (my daughter/niece) and place her in a home to save the marriage. At first I gave in, and we stated interviewing different children's homes for her, but it didn't sit well in my heart and soul. And I then realized that it was the wrong thing to do. If I gave her up to a foster home, then who would she have? How would she feel, that she lost her birth parents, then us? It was a bad plan and a terrible idea. So I fired the guy and went to seek counsel somewhere else. The second psychologist guided me in the right direction and pointed to the correct problem. After I had spoken to him, he brought into light the dysfunctionality in our marriage and relationship.

That's when the psychologist told me that I was suicidal and that I was under more stress, than most guys coming back from war. He said: "Valerio, a funny thing about you Christians. You don't believe in suicide, but you'll act it out".

Boom! It hit me. I denied it all. "No way! Not me. You're f**king crazy Doc!"

After a month of counseling on the couch, we figured out why I was behaving the way I was. It was due to my lousy marriage (relationship with my ex-wife, and not my niece/daughter) and he (Doc) was either going to help me get through it or he was going to help me to get out of it.

 So I chose the latter.

A funny thing happened after we had gotten divorced. My daughters "episodes of rage" started to calm down. She started to chill out and become more relaxed around me. So one day as we were driving home from Nashville (so that she can spend the weekend with me) we started talking (as always) and to my amusement, she told me that she was glad we had divorced.

Here's how our conversation went:

"Why?" I asked

Her answer: "you guys were always fighting with each other. And I was always getting upset with the yelling, and I would sit in my room and cry in my bed. It was so bad that I would call my friend crying, telling her that you guys were fighting again, and I couldn't take it anymore. And she would talk to me and calm me down. Now that you both are divorced and you have your own places, I can stay with mom, and when she is having a bad day and when I need to get away from her, I can come and stay with you, while she relaxes and calms down. Plus I don't have to hear the fighting anymore, and you're both a whole lot better now then you were before".

There you have it…

From the mouth of babes the truth came out. We were her problem, or at least a catalyst to her unacceptable behavior.

My lesson from this whole psychologist experience was, if whatever they're saying doesn't sit right with your heart, pray hard for a new direction and seek a second opinion. Just because they're labeled expert, doesn't mean that they're on the right track. Even professional NASCAR drivers crash every now and then. I'm so glad that I listened to my heart and didn't let go of the joy in my life, my daughter/niece, in exchange for some pseudo tranquility. I'm also glad that I sought the second advice and got to the proper issue, which was my dysfunctional marriage of co-dependency.

We as humans tend to do things backwards sometimes.

Supposedly, boy meets girl, girl likes boy, and they date. They then start a relationship that leads to marriage, sex and children. Not in my case.

My ex-wife and I had dated a few months before I had gotten her pregnant and I decided to do the right thing and marry her. And this was my pattern of behavior: Boy sees girl, lusts for her, has sex, makes baby, marries, and then tries to build a relationship with the stranger. And after my divorce I continued that pattern over and over again. Meet girl, lust, sex, fall in love, then try to know the person and build a relationship. The crazy part about it is that I would met the girl, sin, then tell God to make it all better with that person. Kind of backwards isn't it? What I should have done, was: Meet girl, get to know her, build a friendship, build a relationship, date, get engaged, marriage, sex, walk the beaches of the world.

So here it is, my memoirs and journal in poetry form, with some added letters that we wrote to each other as the heart of the relationship evolved.

How this guy who was a small pillar of the Christian community fell.

Not only did I fall, but I rolled over in a ditch and got caught on the barbwire fence and stood there for a while, in misery, pain and agony in my muddy depression. With broken relationships spewed all around me, as my soul blead out. Then while I was just about to get out of the ditch, a car rolled over my fingers, and a storm hit (just when I thought it couldn't get any worse).

But while lying there in misery, a voice told me to "get up!" Reach up and grab His hand and follow Him once again. And I did.

The good news is that there is a healing God that loves us and forgives our sins, and heals us from our wounds. The biggest struggle for all of us (as humans) is that we are healed, but not restored. (I'm not a bible scholar so bear with me) In the Bible, Mark chapter 5:25-29 there is a woman that was bleeding for 12 years, and her faith lead her to believe that if she touched the cloak of Jesus that she would be healed. And when she did, Jesus stopped and asked the disciples who touched him. Amongst the crowd that had gathered, and were pressing against them, they didn't know. But Jesus did. He stopped and looked around, and she, trembling with fear, told Jesus and the crowd her story. But the clincher lies in verse 34, when he said to her: "daughter, your faith has made you well, go in peace and be healed of you disease". Her faith to be healed was to touch Him. But to be fully restored, she had to confess her sin and faith to Him and the crowd. WOW! Her restoration came in sharing her faith. So here I am healed, and sharing my faith with you in an attempt to restore my life.

Hopefully, I pray that this will give you the hope to be healed and restored, and relay to you that you're not alone. The struggle is real. I'm writing this for you, the guy or girl that has gone or is going through what I went through. Deep depression, failed marriage, an affair, divorce, co-dependency, broken relationships, low self-worth, lack of purpose, topped with a dash of suicidal thoughts.

Let me say that others have gone through all of this before you and I. And they have fallen and gotten back up. There are times when people look at me as if I have the scarlet letter "A" on my chest. So be it! In the famous words of my ex (in her New York accent)"Who cares?" (Pronounced Kay-yars) Let the haters hate and the ones that cast judgment: judge. For they too will be judged by the same measure they judge me. It's none of my business what their thoughts are about me, and my circumstances. They have no skin, scabs or blood in my game of life.

If I can share my history with you, relate with you to help you, and let you know that there is an Almighty God that loves you, and that you don't have to be depressed or co-dependent on someone else for happiness, then I have accomplished His and my purpose for this book. This is why I am opening up my writings, failures, pain and raw feelings to you.

My hope is that you find happiness within yourself. Once you get through your walk in the desert, the happiness and an abundant life await you at the other side.

Just listen to Him, get back up on your feet and move forward towards his voice and follow His plan.

AN AFFAIR IS BORN

It happened.

I met someone who was incredibly sexy.

Her sharp and witty mind, her curvaceous full figured body, her personality and the confident way she carried herself, was mind blowing to me. How in the world would anyone like that want me? I felt like the biggest loser winning the largest Powerball in history. This hot full figured redheaded woman adored everything about me. It was intoxicating!

We were both in bad marriages and we would joke on how we should just swap spouses because our spouses would be great for each other, as we were incredible for each other as well.

It was on the afternoon of July 8.

We had been texting back-and-forth flirtatiously.

Finally I called her and I asked her "…what are we going to do about this massive chemistry that we have?"

Her innocently laced toned, reply was, "I don't know? What are we going to do about it?"

Me, "Well we need to meet and talk. We can't go on like this? This is not right and we need to lay down some rules".

In her sweet Alabamian tone she said "sure! Let's meet behind the small church by my house, I'll send you a text when I get there".

When I got to the parking lot behind the small church, her car was already there. I pulled up beside her car. She was wearing a sundress and her hair was done perfectly. I looked at her and gestured for her to come sit in my car. In the passenger seat she sat quiet for a moment and look to me and said "Hey Valerio, what would you like to talk about."

I undressed her with my eyes, and caught her checking me out top to bottom with a grin on her face. Hot blood started to race throughout my body. I could feel my ears turn flush with heat as my testosterone kicked into high gear. It was as if I were in a fight or flight and my hands started to shake. Still, cool, in a calm voice, I said "about our chemistry…. it's pretty strong. What do you think we should do about it? What do you think?"

Her eyes smiled at me and batted, "You don't want to know what I'm thinking. Or do you? We can talk about whatever you want. What would you like to know?"

My witty mind kicked in, unfiltered, uncensored, boundaries nowhere to be found, the first thought that popped into my head was verbalized in an instinct, "Do you really want to know what I want to know?"

She grinned and said, "uh huh".

"What's beneath that dress?"

Lifting up her dress and exposing her brown laced silky underwear, smiling like a Cheshire cat, she said, "We'll that's easy silly boy." Then she chuckled.

The Latin side in me went into over drive, as if I was going through an out of body experience. My right hand reached over to the back of her neck caressing her long silky red hair, touching and brushing the tips of my fingers by her ears, while my left hand reached down and petted her silky brown underwear and made its ways in and touched a red pelt.

"Oh, a true redhead! How nice." I pulled the hair on the back of her neck. She closed her eyes and I kissed her ears, neck then lips softly without remorse. The untamed, no boundaries, animal side of me kicked in. My fingers explore her inner thighs and she let out

a release that entrenched my hand and the seat of the car.
That's when the affair began. In full tilt, forward, at the speed of lust.

It was seductively secretive and exciting. My animal magnetism (as she called it) and her sassy self (combined) was better than any "Tele Novella" on Spanish TV today.
She called me Bond-007, and "Remmy" (short for Renaissance man) and I called her Redhead (RH) and eventually "Polish Princess" after her favorite drink.

We'd set up dates and met in remote parking lots, cheesy hotel rooms, and restaurants. We talked and texted continuously, flirted audaciously, dreamed big, laughed uncontrollably, and made love intensely for hours at a time. We were just like any super couple that was caught up in a fantasy. It all seemed too perfect, too fast, real deep and extremely powerful. I should've walked away after the first afternoon we met, but I couldn't. She was emotionally and sexually intoxicating. We had broken it off several times, before and after, waiting for our divorces to finalize. But we couldn't let go, no matter how hard we tried. We were co-dependent on each other to get through our divorces. We didn't know how to be alone by ourselves. Nor did we want to be alone by ourselves. Our chemistry was enhanced one hundred fold via sex, our combined magnetism and like thinking. It was as if a humanistic fission had taken place. An explosion that engulfed us and everyone who was around us. An out of control chain reaction of atomic particles, excited beyond recovery, leading us to this explosive sexual affair.
The first chapter of the book is actually a small book that I wrote and had given to her. It's a compilation of poems I had written

and letters we exchanged. During this time, my mother (Naty) had passed away in Puerto Rico. She was severely sick in the hospital, and was bleeding internally. My aunt Rosa had called and said that I needed to come and see her. I called the Redhead (a nurse) and explained to her the symptoms on hand. When I called she was at a luncheon with a group of specialist nurses, who heard the symptoms then told me that she had days to live. They also told me I needed to rush over to Puerto Rico, and see her for the last time before she passed. During that difficult time in my life, my spouse was fighting with me. She demanded that she too fly to Puerto Rico with me to see her. She couldn't. She had a job, my daughter was doing finals in school, and would have missed them flying with us, and we couldn't afford the three one thousand dollar airline tickets to fly there. We were financially maxed out and drowning in debt. When I got there my mother had massive internal bleeding. The doctors she was seeing in Puerto Rico were only treating the symptoms not the issue (according to my doctor and nurse friends). They had let the disease of Leukemia run its course for the past four years. They thought, at eighty four years old, that she didn't need any treatment. So when she was sick, they'd pump new blood into her, then send her home after forty eight hours in the hospital (which was all that Medicare paid for). They also had a rotating staff of doctors who didn't want to take responsibility for her treatment. So who ever was on shift that night would give her a "bandage" solution, then send her home. My step dad Jose did the best he could to take care of her. He left his drinking and bad habits at seventy years old, and started to take care of himself and her. He'd take her to all of her appointments, cook and clean for her, and did the grocery shopping all by himself when she wasn't able to go with him. He was eighty six years old at that time. It was a true storm I had gone through, with my ex-wife yelling at me on the phone, taking care of my grieving father, teaching him how to be alone, and doing the arrangements for my mother's cremation, and the ceremony of scattering her ashes by the brook she washed her cloths in as a child (as she had stated she wanted).

During this time it all started to take a toll on my health. All I wanted to do is sleep. In Puerto Rico I would sleep 10-12 hours a day, as migraines and depression disabled me. But I had to push on and accomplish my mother's wishes, and help my step dad, regardless of what was happening to me.

Here it is, in its entire form, in poetry and letters.

RENAISSANCE MAN

Dear beloved,
The mementos we've stolen together
In our pool of lust and pleasure
Have indeed redefined us
And have opened our hearts and eyes
To a facade of hiding and lies
So to this we both give in
Yes, let's call it Sin!
As if no other man has done
Nor woman has climbed the rung

Your fiery hair impaled my thoughts
To do thing I would have never sought
Your lustful brown eyes coo' d me in
To immerse myself in our flings

My heart is in tears when the thought
Of this "thing" becomes naught
In our memories we'll reminisce our encounters

And in the resting home, we'll both rekindle and remember
Of the time when the *Red Head* met the *Renaissance Man*
In a remote parking lot
Thinking… "of course not"…
And they endeared each other like no modern couple can
With the love and lust that was discarded by others in the can
Someone's husband, another's wife: became lovers
And in un-thoughtful lust they were smothered

So, in remembrance till the day we depart,
Then die,
We'll hold our memories of those flings gone bye
A lockbox in your sacred heart
Opened with only a key, a smile, of your Latin Lover
Your memories will forever last
Of the last...
Renaissance man discovered

EXPLICIT: RH&RM

RH and *RM* were together once again
And played little games of lust and pretend
A meet here for lunch
A peekaboo then a touch,
In front of his wife!
A call, a text
As they traveled through life
They compared their songs
Together reminisced
Of youth and the life
They thought they'd longed
Their meetings violent
With lust and desire
Lasting hours
Their passion on fire
Through their bliss
They persist
A tug of her hair
A grab of her throat
A cold chill
Down the small of her back
Their sex pulsated
As free as the air
A thrust forward
And a reactive scratch
Squeezing kegels
Grasping for more
3 hours gone by

Did they care?
Nevermore!
Now the cuffs come out
And the bad cop is present
The assailant is arrested
And then embedded in it
The naughty girl's then let out
She moans Spanish words
Taught by her lover (To his credit)
The words he once owned
Their plans can't be sought
Because lust is their folly
And if they're caught?
Oh my!
Oh bye-Golly!

EVE'S EVE

So you walked by the passion tree
Guessing it's fruit and how'd it taste
Another person's apple
Hanging ready for the take
Freshly picked
You saw it, said "he's mine"
An apple for your thoughts
Plucked like a grape from a vine

As you bit it
Lust thrashed through your body
Another bite, a chew, a swallow
The church bells started to ring really hollow
In the front seat of his car the first taste left you wanting
Several encounters later *(201)* were real daunting!

With the taste of this fruit your eyes opened Eve
To the sins and the hopes that you thought you'd never seen
"I'm a realist! And I pride myself so…."
Amongst a crowd of people, you find yourself alone
A friend of fine arts, girlfriends dancing to your song
Alone with the apple core, kinky drinks numb it all

*Note: "201" is the number to our first hotel room. And 201 is also the
famous address to the Memphis jail house, 201 Poplar Ave.*

11AM

11am, too far away from now.
Almost an eternity.
How I long to hear your voice Right here, standing still....
Waiting for you, with withered flowers in my hands.
Cold, alone, high with hope and anticipation.
A warm withering spot in my heart,
That only u can touch, is waiting....

To be re-ignited.
And feed, with your kisses
Adoration, is the hearts whisper....
For a touch ¡llamame!
Querida, querro sientir su amor

Remmy

MA JOURNEE VIDE

My day is empty, "tu me manques"
I just wanted to hear your voice "Une minute"
Tears swell in my eyes, "au moment où j'ecris ce mail"
Yea, what a tough man!
Everywhere I go; there is a "memoire"
McAlester's, Macy's, Millano's...
I hope you don't hate "moi"
"Adieu mon amour"

Remmy

LETTER & POEM:

P: Ok so I woke up at 4 and just got on my phone and you're typing. Weird.

R: Yes I agree. She would feel your vibe and think something is up. I just woke up and am getting ready to go to work. But I can't stop fighting the tears for the deep love I have for you. I really, really miss us. And hope that time leaps forward so that we would meet again faster.

P: We're connected.

R: You're my love my heart.

P: Yes we are very connected! I have tears too but I know in my heart it's all going to be ok. I was thinking I need this time to heal from my divorce too - all those wasted years all 4 of us will be better off for taking this time in the long run. <3

R: I know in my brain.... But my heart "no speaks-a da language". I'm going to eat breakfast then leave.

Sleep sweet my love.

P: You make me smile. Ok baby <3

R: I love your new pic.

I'm so in love with you.
A breath (without you near) is cheap air.
This is truly an epic battle of the soul and heart, fighting off the evils of day's gone bye.
And now as the battle withers, the time to save the wounded, and say good bye to the dead has come upon us. Heal sweet soul, heal.
Lay thee slumber in your angel's arms, rest thine eyes and calm thee spirit. For when we wake, our wounds would be healed and our spirits refreshed, to be united as one. Rest my love, and cast

thy sorrow to the slumbering winds. For when we awake, together
our souls will be.
Remmy

I don't check this email that frequently but I just checked it and you
had just sent this. We are so in sync. No way is this relationship ever
going away. I will wait for you...you are absolutely worth any sacrifice
I have to make...update me on your personal progress sometime
although I will probably know how you are, I will just feel it...
PP/RH

LETTERS:

My teary heart requests the photos of you.
RM

I keep reading your email and poetry you have sent me over the past months; I wish I could write you something so passionate and beautiful. Your words really touch my soul, as do you. I am so thankful we are able to talk so openly and honestly and resolve our issues such as we did today. I never ever want to hurt you or shut you out of my life. I love you with all my being and never dreamed I would ever have anyone as wonderful as you in my life. You are my One in a Million too!

Love,
RH

So... It's Christmas Day, the day you tell the important people in your life how much they mean to you so I wanted to tell you more than anyone else in the world Merry Christmas and that I love you. I hope your day is wonderful and I wish we were together today laughing and holding each other...
Merry Christmas!
All My Love,
RH

I just wanted to say hi, I miss us.
Lunch is lonely without you.
Your smile, laugh, and silly lisp to the right corner or your mouth, still fogs my mind.

I sit at our booth, and my eyes wonder to the door to see if you're coming in, and my sense of scent is heightened, searching for your smell.

Adios mama,

Hasta later.

Remmy

A SWING IN TIME

As we wait for time, to pass us by
And test the metal that we are made of
I dream a dream, of us on our front porch
On the wooden swing hanging from the ceiling
At the house that love built
With your head in my lap, eyes closed breathing softly
My beloved asleep, with sweet drool from your lips

And I with pen and pad in hand
Metaphors, meter, conceit
Flowing with my feathered pen
As my fingers touch your rich rusty red hair
Hyperboles, enjambments, haikus
Detangling your dreams
Alliterations, assonances, onomatopoeia
Zooming through my mind
Stanza, sonnet, similes,
Slithering silently on the sheets
Step by step as you sleep

Through my eyes
I ingest
The beauty of your slumber
And personify on sheet, your angelic presence

And to Father Time I would profess
That if the world were large enough
And eternity had time to spare

I'd spend centuries adoring
Each part of my beloved's body
And strands of hair.
Remmy

MY HEART IS IN SORROW

Letter & Poem:

I've read and re-read our poems and letters to each other. And I feel blessed that we have found each other, in this faceless sea of people... My heart is also filled and refilled every time we're together. Please understand that I am struggling with an old world paradigm mind set. I also wish to leave her and my daughter in the best finical, emotional and physical shape possible. My heart aches & longs to be with you. You ARE truly my soul mate, that chance and fate has personified itself before me. Thank you, my love for being strong when I am weak, and for seeing what I am not able to view. Shortly our hearts will beat as one, and we will share the same bed. Thank you for loving me and being patient. You will be repaid with eternal happiness and comfort in my arms.
Remmy

My heart is in sorrow.
My mind is limp
Without your stimulation.
Pain, sorrow, loneliness
Personify themselves with every tear.
I'm alone.
And can't bear it.
The darkness is too consuming,
Where are you my beloved?
Safe I pray.
Wait for me at the edge of this darkness
Where this loneliness, sorrow and pain will reside.

Call my name.
So that I may follow the sweet southern sensuous sound of you
voice.
Lead me out.
Please save me from this sorrow, loneliness and pain.

Remmy

LETTERS:

Thanks for the message. Save yourself. It's the only way to live a healthy, happy life... I'm in the process of taking care of me! Talk to you March 1st.
RH

I've read, and reread you previous emails (all of them).
And I am sorry for any pain that I have caused you.
That was never my intention. If not, the opposite of that were my intentions.
To cause you joy and happiness, with what little I can give you in a moment's notice.
I will respect your wishes as much as my heart allows me to.
The 1st 24-48 hrs has been the hardest for my soul to bear, without its soul mate.
I'm lonely and afraid. I find it hard to exist, even without your friendship.
You complete and compliment me.
I just read your message. Heal my love. For I bear enough pain for both of us.
March 1st can never get here fast enough. Pray that the house sells immediately.
RM

Falling, **FAILING,** falling

I tumble, twitch, and turn
Cold sweat drips down my brow
Fiery chills, flash through my soul
Tremors of pain
Relief when gone
Hands cringing, fists locked, toes curled
Head cock, eyes slam shut when inflicted
Left nostril sniffs the air searching for your fragrance
The taste of your lips still lingers on the tip of my dry numb tongue
Your light touch, replaced by a wrecking ball shattering through my body
I ponder getting up. I'm hurt, I cringe
           I fall, FAIL to get up. Fall again
I'm distressed, doomed, done
Come back, my darling, inject your venom into my soul
Through thy eyes. Methadone
Reduce my pain, and slow the tears that drain my existence
Relieve me every 4 hours, or as needed
Your presence, a guise, a soft beam from thy thin lips
I'm now shut out, cut off by thee....
"Owe, Pain, agony!"
         I'm falling, FAILING to get up, falling again
Wicked Windy whispers
Crescendo through my head
The last time you said
"Valerio".
Why did you let me go
A soft silent pounding presence

Pouring through my frontal lobe
      I'm falling, FAILING to get up, falling again.
Dying, detoxed, decomposed, heart
Exposed through an old open chest wound
Silently slowing its pace
Thumping unconsciously through time
Red fluid drains from its core
Removed from my body
Ravaged in obscurity
"Ugh, aye, Dolor!"
      I'm falling, FAILING to get up, falling again.
Tossed, turning towards
That heart shaped mass
Now airborne onto a landfill of burning biohazards
I'd prayed you'd be around
Before it'd hit the ground
To catch it, in your grasp
"Ay DIOS! Grab it!"
"Save meeee!"
      From falling, FAILING, falling again.

Remmy

My PPP

My polished princess perceives
That life would bear better without me
Now my mind is blocked
Because my luscious lustful love is all I've got
To inspire my writings
To feel her presences is delighting
But now as my purple plumed pen goes cold
Feelings wither in my soul
And lead replaces the gold
My heavy hurting heart grows numb
The look on my face becomes dumb
And my thoughts expire
Like flowering flowing flames above a fire
Before they record on paper
Thoughts become vapor
Like a destitute desolate desert calling the rain
My heart calls my honey again
To rejuvenate my brain
And to help me sustain substantial sentences,
To finish…

RM

LETTER AND POEM LETS LIVE

LETTERS:

Where's my poem?
So... No kik, no poem, no love letter. What's up Remmy? Not like you... You ok over there?
RH

I miss u my lovely.
RM

Which is more important inhaling or exhaling? RM
Laughter and love intertwine and are equally as important as breathing. RH

LET'S LIVE
You're my splash of color
In this black and white world
A whirl of sanity
Clarity, in this crazy crisis
My liberator
The love of my life
A question I behold to thee hereafter
A veil to uncover thereafter
Is love inhaling and laughter exhaling?
Or the other way around
Or are they both bound
To my amazement, you reply:
"Love, inhaling because you take it in and it fills up", as when my

lovely fills my cup!
"Laughter exhaling because it's a release".
As when a sheep gives up its fleece!
Then my lovely stands
With a grand ovation
<Gesturing with her hand>
"God, I love our Conversations!"
And that is what makes *US* grand.

Remmy

LETTER AND POEM "I JUST WANTED"

Sexy pic of you and your Labios I love to kiss. Yes the short amount of time this afternoon was wonderful except for you leaving. The intimacy was spectacular. I am glad I was there for you and always want us to be like that. If I could have one wish granted it would be to fast forward time until we are together and then to make time stand still. Good night to the love of my life and the only man I adore.
RH

You + Me/ ASAP = my priority.
RM

Bet you are sleeping so well with your Ambien. Obviously, I have not taken mine...because I am up thinking about and writing you... hope you behaved with your Ambien on board. I certainly don't... but we will save that for an all-nighter.

Sent by an Absolutely Marvelous Sender RH

I just wanted to let u know,
I'm really gonna miss our fun time together this coming
week.
Fri & Sat have been a struggle.
My mind is mush,
Sorry no poem.
I have no push
Can I get some on loan?
For a well deserving poem.
Adios Mama.
Remmy

I hate the way you had to leave today and that we couldn't steal away for some more time together - but the time we did have was remarkable. I enjoyed every minute especially falling asleep with your arms wrapped tight around me. Nothing has ever felt so peaceful and good. Let me know how things are going with you and when I can see my lover again...

Sent by an Absolutely Marvelous Sender RH

Oh my polished princess!
How I long to be with thee this evening.
Separated by space and words, our souls continue as one.
Our common goal is clear, together explore and travel the world.
Our hearts beat in sync, to the drum steps of our inner music.
Be with me now my love and let time not pass us by.

Remmy

MEMPHIS SLANG

It says u are down to earth.....
Or should I Memfrican-ize and says Urf?
Describes u to a tee,
My PP.
Did u read?
Da pic's descript I sent to thee?
Ov dee description,
Ov dee ocular infliction
Ov da pics provided,
Purple swirl was what caught my eye.
But ov course,
Dee green swirl,
Threw dee Irish girl,
Off course.

AM I A FREAK?

Of the question if you're a freak,
My princess know the answer she seeks
Bondage Pain Pleasure
Are the common main treasures
That she hopes to boast
As she's tied, spanked, and blind folded

To her bed post.

Remmy

I'M UP.

I've been up all night.
A dispute,
A fight!
A million things racing through my head.
About what was said and not said.
About what was done wrong?
And what was done right.
As the night lingered the bells tolled.
About my wealth accumulated
Then all the things got sold.
About the cleansing of my conscious and my soul.
Do I stop and fold.
Or do I continue and be bold
And be sold
On the idea
Of freedom lost
Was time well spent?
For the freedom of my soul
In future events.

Call me when you get up
Because even though I'm up
I've been up
But haven't been able to get up
From being down

Remmy

CALL ME AMOR

Call me Amor

I want to hear your soothing lovely voice in my ear.

I miss the smell of your breath in the morning.

Your tangle hair and the sand in your eye.

To me you personify

The true essence of beauty,

and I am engulfed in it.

MY PRETTY PEARL

Where art tho my PP?
Does thy heart still skip for me?
Does thy mind delight with memories of my touch?
And thy vagina elate euphorically with moisture?
Like a red bearded Oyster...
A very rare species-what not...
Found in the deepest of lochs
Where no Croc
Has dared to swim,
Because Nessie still roams within.
Like her (Nessie) your presence a mystery,
But unlike her I know thy history
in thy Oyster a pearl so white
When my tongue touches thy pink lips
I bite.
And eject?
Oh how it does!
Thy pearliest sweet nectar sends me abuzz
And thy throbbing hips do send home
Thy pleasures crescendos with thy moans.

WHY IS IT WHEN I RIDE MY HARLEY

Why is it when I ride my Harley
Little boys race me on their bike
Old people pull aside in their cars
Guys hold their girlfriends tighter
Ladies smile
And little girls wave?
Damn, I love this bike!

RH: You look so hot on your bike. I just hate the sad look on your face. Hugs and kisses to my Remmy.

RM: Thank you my love. Biking Remmy.

This poem is dedicated to Natividad Henriquez Crespo. The light of my life, and the coolest, most marvelous mother a boy/man can ever have. I love you dearly, and life will never be the same without your touch, smile and laughter. Rest in Peace my beautiful love. I'll see you in heaven.

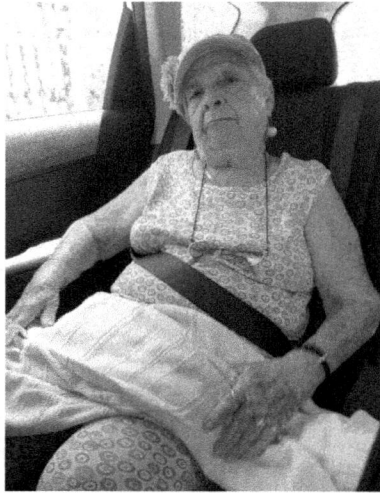

My mom, old school gangster.

OF ALL THE THINGS IN LIFE

Of all the things in life
the best I remember was
when she held my hands tight.
In the end, a fate we all will share,
when we leave this Earth,
Who would really care?
Cars, homes, material things you can't take,
Will not fit in your box,
Because one size is all they make.
A few pounds of ashes in a neat black box,
I picked up from Lajas Memorial,
around 4 o'clock.
Things she said raced through my mind,
"When I'm gone, don't worry, I'll be fine".
"Let them keep their flowers and sorrow,
That crap won't add a minute to my tomorrows,
Don't come to see that my soul has left,
Time waits for no one,
Not the sick nor even the dead..."
Her lessons I've learned, and memories I keep,
I repeat, repeat,
until they seep.
T'was the night of Christmas
84 years ago,
Natividad Henriquez Pabon
was born, on an island, with no Santa, reindeers or snow.
The only mother I had,
who I loved and known,

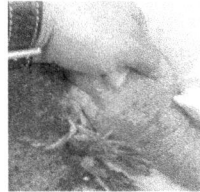

Adopted me in May, 48 years ago.
Now forward in time we go.
This question I dare, during your dash of life what burdens did
you bear?
Was your story a legacy of wisdom, compassion and love,
or will you be forgotten,
like an old pair of gloves?

Sleep your eternal sleep,
my beautiful mother,
you will never be forgotten

Don't worry, please sleep,
I'll take care of father

Your son
Valerio

CHAPTER 2

Corazones Roto se rompen
(Broken Hearts are broken)

BROKEN

As Humphrey Bogart said, "We'll always have Paris". (Casablanca).

The Polished Princess and I would always have "The epic affair".

We were no longer together. After a few years of going through our divorces, the drama from our spouses, breaking up, then getting back together again in pursuit of a fantasy romance, going on vacations to the Caribbean, little towns in the Ozarks, we were done. As we were driving back from a trip to Dallas TX. I wrote the "3 shots" song as a bet that I can write a country song before we got back home.

Like any new relationship, there were a lot of misunderstandings, hurt feelings miscommunications, private topics, feelings and insecurities (aka: "elephants in the room") that we wouldn't talk about, that tore us apart. We loved each other intensely, but we didn't trust each other with our emotions and feelings anymore. There were issues that were still raw from our divorces. And sometimes the only thing that could heal hurt is separation and isolation. We also had to learn how to break the co-dependencies we had with each other, so that we can heal as a whole within ourselves.

I didn't see that back then, but now, after the fact, it's all clear.

We would always have the good memories of days gone by (like Delta Dawn). But our past bad experiences with each other and other people in our lives could never be our present, nor future.

Co-dependent, afraid to be alone and apart, we held on with everything we had. But the chemistry and the sex were not enough to keep us together. So we went on our separate ways in utter disbelief and in massive pain. At least I was.

I tried my best to win her back, telling her how much I had changed, but every time we got together, the "elephants in the room" would come out, and were difficult to discuss and comprehend. It was as if we weren't speaking the same language anymore.

And so, I did my best to move on and establish other relationships with other women. With a plan of the type of women I wanted. She had to be successful at what she did, finically fit (or have a financial plan of some sort), be witty, sexy, educated, healthy, physically fit and well versed in music. Yes, I'm very picky. There were several that were duds, catfishes (not what they looked like on their profiles. As if I wouldn't figure that out when we met!) And lame. I had coffee, dinner and even took the exceptional ones to my favorite hangouts. But the majority of them didn't interest me. Nothing against them, they were all really nice and pretty, but they didn't reignite the chemistry I once had and was looking for.

I was beside myself, as if I had to prove to myself that there were more fish in the sea. The Polished Princess wasn't the only one that could fit the "soul mate" hole I had in my heart.

Depressed and fighting co-dependency, I struggled with these relationships and my relationship with God. Actually I had given up my relationship with God, on several occasions.

The fireworks and the excitement from the previous relationships were incredible, but now rang hollow. I felt soulless. All the ladies I dated said the same thing, "You're so much fun and exciting!" And that would continue to be my downfall.

I had set no boundaries on myself, and I allowed ME to run unfiltered, full throttle, with no reservations and not a care in the world. My feelings were on my sleeves, I had my poetry pen in one hand, and the emotional IQ of a Jr. High School jock in the other, with zero expectations as to what I really wanted in a relationship.

It was fun but it wasn't reality. And the ladies I dated had some of the greatest times of their lives (as they had told me). We pulled some all-nighters going out, dancing, dining, going to shows, and making love.

I was funny, fun, had money, time, freedom and ability to express myself, and most importantly, I acted like a real man. Most of the guys I heard about were major duds, and or losers, with zero personalities or couth on how to treat or romance a lady. In the dating pool, I had them beat. Or maybe not.

I knew I couldn't keep this up for long. It was completely reckless, and the reality of it is that I wasn't the party boy everyone had me out to be.

One day on a dare (at the local craft beer place) my friends challenged me to meet random girls. I'm always up for a good challenge, so they pointed to a table where two ladies sat, and the guys dared me to go and talk to them. So I took my beer and walked over to the table and introduced myself. I figured, a definite "no" would be not to ask, so I asked them if I could join them. They said," Sure but there's no chair here." so I went back to my table grabbed my chair (winked at my buddies) and sat with the ladies for the rest of the night. We talked, drank a few beers and laughed at the dumbest things we could come up with. All three of us had a sarcastic witty banter conversation going on that would make grandma pee in her depends. That's when I met a very interesting brunette who was pursuing her MBA. She was a single mom raising boys, working full time, while getting her degree. Our one to one conversations were deep, a little sarcastic and funny. She peaked my interest and got my attention. I really wanted to know more about her. So I gave her my number on a piece of paper and said "Here's my number. I'm not going to put any pressure on you by asking you for yours, but if you ever want to meet again, feel free to text me or call me. I'd really like to hear from you again". After that I left and sat back down with the guys and had another drink as she and her girlfriend got up and left. A week went by and I didn't hear from her.

On a Friday afternoon I was looking at a dating app and I came across her photo. And I texted her via the app, "Are you stalking me?" which lead to some funny comeback's and hilarious texting, back and forth. The truth was she was looking for me via the app, and she had misplaced my number in her book bag. We started conversing on the app which led to a date the next day. The date went exceptionally well with a hit to third base (for all of you baseball fans). I wrote a poem about it.

I had gotten my mojo back and felt like I was going to be all right. But my depression kept eating at me (as you can read in this chapter). After hitting a home run on the second date, and dating her for about a week she decided that we weren't a fit. She had two dogs that kept jumping on me and driving me crazy every time I sat next to her on her couch. They wanted her attention and didn't like the idea of momma having a stranger in the house. It annoyed the heck out of me, and she could see it. Yes we had gotten intimate, we didn't have chemistry, but it was nice having someone to talk to, be friends with and have fun with. I wanted to continue our cozy friendship but it was DOA (dead on arrival) after the dogs' incident. We had texted back and forth after the breakup, but it wasn't like before. I had seen her once or twice at the craft beer place, and we said hello a few times, and we kept it cordial, playful and cool. So that was the end of that relationship.

The break up didn't bother me that much, until later on that night.

That little piece of rejection, was the tipping point that threw me deep into the pit of depression. I was at the point where I called my friend Amy and ask her to talk to me, and be with me, because I was feeling horrible as if I wanted to die. I didn't know why I was feeling this way, and it scared me.

I know some of you can relate to this (at some point of your life), it was a real shitty feeling. Unlike the IDGF (I don't give a F*) attitude when I had my bike. The pit seemed deeper, and the darkness came to life swallowing me entirely alive. Here I was in the belly of a beast, alone asking for help.

Here is that part of my pain of loneliness and co-dependency in poetry form.

THREE SHOTS TWO BEERS
ONE STEP FROM LOVING YOU

I was going from Nash-Vegas to Texas
When I stopped over in Memphis
On my way to Beale, I parked my Peterbilt by the Peabody
With my four ways on
Humming this country song
I looked in the "Flying Saucer"
And I saw her
A beer nerd
From Billy Bob's honky-tonk
Down in the Dallas bonkey donk
And that's why
I'm 3 shots, 2 beers, 1 step from loving you...

With your smile of malice
And a spunk like Alice
From Mel's diner
That's why I had to find 'er.
You set me on fire
Like Richard Pryor.
And that's why
I'm 3 shots, 2 beers, 1 step from loving you...

I got a 5 gallon Stetson
A four dollar puck of sniff
And a three dollars of chew root
To get me through this haul
But this stop I had to do

To meet a gal like you,
Baby you beat them all.
And that's why
I'm 3 shots, 2 beers, 1 step from loving you...

Girl, why do you make me feel like this?
Like the Stylistics
You make me feel brand new.
And I'm doing things I shouldn't do.
I'm shackled by your eyes and you by mines.
Your look has me hypnotized.
And my Stetson has you mesmerized.
I'm intoxicated by your laughter.
And now it's me you're after.
And we're both weakened by our touch.
And that's something we can't fuss.
That's when you were
3 shots, 2 beers, and 1 dance from loving me…

AD: RENAISSANCE MAN
SEEKS RENAISSANCE WOMAN.

Dear possible Beloved,
My aim is straight,
I'm high on my Plateaus,
I've assumed a quest,
Like Menelaus!
I have search hidden ancient maps,
And I've launched a thousand ships and apps,
To find and retrieve, my very own Helen of Troy.
A Beauty so grand, a strand of her hair,
Would unglue any common man, with incredible joy.

Be tho she?
Let us see.
My desires include,
That, which I pursue,
A succulent bust, able to contain the greatest of hearts,
Who would not discard this Romantic's art.
She must be able to love unconditionally like Lucy and Ricky,
Be we in situations, dirty or sticky.
For the pervious lady's heart was blurred,
(As I heard, it smelled misty, like rubble).
If she would have known Katie and Hubbell
In "The Way We Were".
She'd understand, "When you love someone… you go deaf, dumb
and blind."
For if she did, it would've resounded within her mind.
Back to the needed be,

Her beauty undisputed like Cleopatra!
Her grace be her mantra.
And like the Bridges of Madison County,
I would be your Robert. Can you play Francesca?
Photos of you? "Si, que Bella!"
Witty Conversations like George had with Gracie,
About nations, gorges and cities,
For those who would hear us would think we were crazy.
And if time rewinds and either memory fail,
I'll be your Noah to Allie (The Notebook), and I'd read you Our
Tale.
Ahh Lady that I seek,
My reason is clear,
You can be my Grace Kelly
And I, your Prince Rainier!

You see, for I truly believe:
"Success is nothing without someone to share it with"
(Mahogany),
For that I hold no apology!!

For I am the Last Renaissance man,
Whom wants to live and someday die,
hand in hand,
With the last Renaissance woman,
By my side.

Sincerely yours,
The Last Renaissance man Alive
Remmy901

TREND

I see a trend with all the women I date
I make them feel loved
They like my strong arms
They feel safe around me and when I hug them
They love my communication
They enjoy the ability that I touch them physically
They like that I look into their eyes when they speak to me
They like that I speak my mind and have my own opinion
They like that I'm a tough guy with a soft inside
They see that I'm a man and NOT a metrosexual or a hipster
They enjoy the fact that I like music and the arts and know how to
dance
They like that I take care of my body and eat well
They like that wherever I go I have friends or to make friends I'm
easy to speak with and to
They like the fact that I take care of myself (appearance and body)
They say I'm smart
They say I'm very charismatic
They say that me speaking to them and they speaking to me comes
very natural
They say that when I touch them, it's electric
They say that their body craves my body (primitive instinct)
They say that I'm very romantic
They say that I seize the moment
They say that I know what to say at the right time to get them to
do whatever I want
I say I'm fun and energetic
And thoughtful

I'm protective and they like it
I'm funny
I'm witty
They love my smile
When I look at them their worries melt away
They like that I can handle my finances
That I have money and a good job and a nice house
I have a very big heart
I'm also a nice guy
I'm very understanding
I'm interesting and full of stories
My life experiences are so great that I should write a book
And they all refer to me as "their hot Latin lover"

The funny thing is that I don't consider myself any of that.
I'm just a real man, with feelings, convictions and an opinion, who
loves women.
Go figure.

ECHOES OF HER MOANS

Echoes of her Moans
Crescendo through my head
I lie along in my bed
And the words that she said
Repeat repeat repeat
With a rhythm
Of every
Beat beat beat
Personified
Our love making
Heat heat heat
I lay awake
'cause I can't
Sleep sleep sleep
It moves me
Deep deep deeper
In a trance
I'm trying hard not to see
see see her
As I stare into the air
I can breathe breathe breathe her
Scented Soul in D&G G G
Light blue blue blue
Her love's so true true true
What is a man to do do do
Her image to my left
I go to touch her.....

She left.

IN A DESOLATE DESERT

In a desolate desert
Hangs my heart
Like Dali's clock
Persistently melting,
Surreally perishing
My body lies near
In a shallow grave
Its scraps excavated
By the local wake
Winged Cerberus, Typhon, & Griffon
Silently go through the tattered meat
Alone with my bones
I lie there looking up at them
numbed
by their encroaching pain
Her last great memory gained
rotting in this feast
devoured by these beasts
Only to be passed through quick

Smelling like s**t

MY HEART IS SHATTERED

My heart is shattered
Tattered
Worn
Not worth a whim
Or why
Why did a perfect love
Fail?
Was it frail?
Faulty?
Fruitlessly Founded?
Under Funded?
On borrowed time?
Or emotions?
Was it her smile?
Laughter and dance?
That led to the notion
of an endless romance
I've traveled miles across an ocean
And an unlimited distance
Lies between us
A universe so wide apart
Swallows the pieces

Of my shattered heart

AS A NEWBORN

As a newborn
I learned how to walk
From the carpet
I progressed to dirt
Cement and asphalt
Through life I wondered.
As I raced through the road of life
There were times I'd pick up speed
Slow down, stop and go again
During my quick assent through life, off of the road
I became scared and started running
In my confidence I ran out of cadence with God
Feet stumbling before me
Running roughshod
I fell on graveled road
Rolled down the ditch, through a thorn bush
Stopped by a barbed wired fence
The pain and suffering was extremely intense
I could have stayed there but a whisper told me to move
get up and got back on the road again
And do as I was told
To carry my load
And that God had a purpose and great things ahead
Not to worry about the blood I bled
Nor the tears I'd shed
Only if I continued would I behold these miracles
Blessings so huge they'd almost be Biblical
Slowly, with extreme prejudice against the pain

As I got up again-frayed
I continued down the road

'till this very day

HE REACHED OUT ON THE WEB

He reached out on the web:
Two wounded souls
Converge at a crossroad
Scares bold, incomplete
Like a crossword puzzle.

No clues or codes to unfold
Just some emotions to withhold
Because of previous meets
With people full of rubble.

To his amazement,
He met her in person before
He saw her perpendicular to the door
So he reached out on the web

And said,
"Don't I know you from the Flying Saucer?"
We spoke of Clouds, art, poetry and possibly Chaucer
My number I gave to you that night, you still have it? Am I right"?

"Yes" she said, "it's in my bag,
Underneath my books, and a I think a mag"
"Ok, you have mines
Now what's yours".

She retorted as if he opened a door,
"Just so you know, the old....

I've shown you mine,
Now show me yours...

Doesn't work quite quickly with me"
She texted onto the screen.
Moving fast I replied with a witty remark.
Call me, texting I hate.

Cause I'm old school,
And to his amusement her text continued to flow
"Wow, not too much grass grows under your feet!
I'm awkward on the phone

I prefer to text not speak."
I'm old school I hate to text
But rather talk.
Maybe we can meet? Or go for a walk?

And they did.

WELCOME TO THE LIFE
OF THE BROKEN HEARTED

Welcome to the life of the broken hearted
Where dreams never finished
Only started
Where Tears of fear water the flowers
Of the fainthearted
And memories of sorrow
Obstruct our paths through tomorrow
The sounds of hearts breaking echo through the night
Like crickets waking from an endless plight.
A grey hue for the sky
No sun, moon or stars at night
A colorless barren landscape
With no paths for the forsaken
To use for escape.
No hope, no parades of ticket tape
Only sad memories that play over in our minds.....

....like an unfocused videotape.

IN THIS CROWDED ROOM

In this crowded room
I stand alone
Lonely
Barren of emotions
Like a broken stone
Love avoids me
Like a fleeing leopard
I'm lost without a shepherd.

Surrounded by
the sound of sequence,
the exotic scents of women
and the laughs of establish men.
Sipping their wine and champagne
whispering, about their latest purchase of a corporate plane.
Politics, handshakes and deals ablaze
I'm standing here, elbows to elbow, in my daze.
Will I ever find her?
She that can fill this hole?
I ponder the though and think…
It numbs me.
I pour another drink.

Sip…
…..that's cold.

CHAPTER 3

Luz de mi Corazon
(Heart Light)

BREAKING DEPRESSION

In the deep black storm of depression, I called my best female friend (BFF) Amy again.

She calmed me down and after a few hours of talking on the phone I was able to go home take an Ambien and go to sleep. Before I went to sleep I got back on the dating app and started looking again.

I saw this lady that was pretty and had a very intelligent write up on her app profile. So I texted her a hello, shut the app, went to sleep. That night, faced down on the bed in tears, I was crying to God and asked him to take this depression and pain away. Begging him to help me find someone that I can talk to, be with and enjoy my life with. I fell asleep crying in my prayers, and woke up praying. Praying for death to take me away to ease the pain.

Has that ever happened to you?

That morning I received a reply from this gorgeous girl with green eyes I had said hello to the night before. And we started to text back and forth.

It was a Saturday morning when I broke the "hello" barrier and we set the date for breakfast Sunday morning (the next day) at the local Panera place in Cordova. I don't waste any time when it comes to meet ups.

That Saturday midday, I received a text then a call from my female BFF. She and my Navy buddy were going to take me out to Overton Square to have a great time and to get me out of my depression. It was truly a whirlwind and epic night. We hopped from bar to bar at Overton Square and ended up at a craft beer place in Cordova (leaving with shots they drank, because I was the designated driver). I dropped my Navy pal off at his house, and Amy and I then finish the night in Waffle House at 2 AM. I took her home before daylight, because I had to get up at eight to meet the green eyed girl at 9am. At the Panera, I arrived first, and ordered coffee and a Danish. When I turned around I saw this extremely beautiful redheaded woman with these gorgeous, giant green eyes. Her beauty was stunning and I almost fell back on my feet with shock and awe. She looked at me and said on a soft tone, "Hi!" This was the girl I was supposed to meet, and she recognized me from my profile picture. She wore a black spaghetti strapped shirt with a black knit shirt over it, and dangling ring earrings (which I think looked extremely sexy, which is the New York Rican side of me), with these little square frameless glasses, and her hair was red and curly let loose. She looked ten times better and sexier in person than her profile picture. The opposite of a catfish. A fluke maybe?

We sat at an outside table and chatted for a while, while we had coffee. Yes, the air was full of electricity, excitement and atomic chemistry. My testosterone was peaking again, and my leg started to shake. I was beside myself praising Jesus the whole time. Who was this gentle person? Where did this divine being come from? What the hell is she doing with a schmuck like me? I wanted to know everything about her and absorb every detail that she was willing to give me about her life. I was completely into her: beauty, smile, charisma and the way she handled herself. She was in her mid-thirties and had a gentle Southern charm with a little bit of country and a whole lot of class.

By trade she was a professional violinist, who was going to school during the day, and taking care of her children by herself. She was well-educated, was a great mom, caregiver and financially savvy with the little she scraped up. Her great looks and charm were second to none, and her soft gentle, caring personality kept me homed and locked in. She too had just gone through a divorce several months back, and her wounds and insecurities were still fresh (Wont you ever learn Valerio!!!).

Our relationship took off like a rocket destined to the moon. The first month we spent 27 days out of 30, together. We were intense. The nights that she stayed over, she would cook breakfast, lunch or dinner when she didn't want to go out.

One afternoon, after intense love making, we fell asleep. I was single so I didn't have much in the pantry. When she woke me up, she had a huge meal laid out on the table, topped off with desert. I asked her," Did you go to the store?" She replied with a smile, "No. You had flour and a few things in the pantry that helped me make you this meal from scratch."

Boom! I was blown away. And her food tasted better and was healthier than any high end restaurant I had ever eaten in. I hit the jackpot with her, and it felt awesome! I was walking on sunshine, and tipping the moon. We were in sync at times, thinking of the same things. I'd start a sentence and she'd finish it. It was completely amazing. We never ran out of things to talk about, and we exposed our deepest feelings and fears to each other. We were both wounded from our previous relationships, and our scars still bleed.

After a while we had pet names for each other. I'd call her Tabby, and she called me MD (for reasons I cannot disclose).

One time we had a get together at my house, with some of my friends. I had told Tabby that I loved and missed Puerto Rican water bread. I described how soft and sweet it was, and how out of habit, I usually stopped at the local bakery store in Puerto Rico, I'd pick up a loaf, on the way home while driving on the "Autopista" and eat it in the car. When the party started, she had Water bread in the oven. <<WHAT? >> She had looked it up on YouTube, and got the directions on how to make it, and made it for the party. << AMAZING! >> My coworker who attended the party tasted the bread and said, "Val, where did you buy this bread? Oh my God, it's awesome. I've never had anything like it!" I told him that Tabby had baked it that morning for the party. His reply was blunt and to the point, "Dude! Marry her NOW! I'm not kidding."

I felt as if the Lord has blessed me completely with an "all bases-loaded" home run at the ninth inning.

And as you read on, this entire chapter (and then some) of poems and emails we exchanged, are dedicated to her. Like my previous relationships, we both had scars that had to heal. And only time alone and focus on oneself was the solution. We cared deeply for each other and we were on and off again. But when we were on, it was full throttle. She had named our relationship a "fantasy that was addicting". She had also told me that when times were hard for her while we were apart, she just wanted to say "f**k it!" and call me to be back into her life because everything seemed easier with me around. But she couldn't do that to me. Play with my emotions. She had told me that I was the most caring, giving, and awesome guy she had ever met. But she had started school, as well as was taking care of herself and her kids, and I was a big distraction to her healing and her goals. She was fending for her and her kid's future, and a relationship didn't seem appropriate at this time. It all was over whelming to her. So we ended it with both of us in tears and our hearts shattered. It was the right thing to do. We had tried to be friends, but once you cross the line with someone, anything you do, or try not to do, always leads back to bed. So we had to separate and stay away from each other while continuing with our lives and meet other people. I felt as if she was the right person for me, and I for her, a perfect fit. But the timing was off for both of us.

Until this day I still have triggers of the fantastic times we spent together. But I have to set them aside, and thank the Lord for giving me those moments of pure joy with her. She and her kids will always have a special place in my heart. I wish them nothing but extreme success and happiness.

And as Paul Harvey says, " ...and now for the rest of the story."

TABBY MY QUEEN

Oh my teal Queen
With duel colored eyes of blue and green
My Celtic Venus
Bound by no dominus
My concherto of beauty and grace
No mortal man can embrace.

Milky skin, like a flowering Bennett
My "lady Tennant"
A soft smile that is always present
A priceless jewel among stones
Which, Stradivarius would love to clone.
Cast aside by a mere charlatan,
Perhaps a Corsican.

imposteur de l'amour
ne voit-il pas la fleur

Now mending in my bed
Discarding ill words he once said
haut sur ma pedistal
heures passées qui étaient Epocal
Teal yeux et les cheveux de cuivre
Statuest comme un modelo de Miro
Sieste dans les bras de vous beau
Dreams of days to come
Slumber my sweet
may our dreams be one.

MY KITTY TABBY

My kitty Tabby
is a naughty kitty
When teased will attack!
So I treat it nice, pet it
and kiss it back
This kitty is a red and pretty
country kitty
Crimson and blonde fur
When I stroke her, she purrs
And when I tease her, she fights
nails down my back, all through the night
This Ginger tabby
when happy
Purrs and meows
in a French accent, "miaou!"
And when in heat
she's not discreet
about the pleasure she seeks
And at the peak of her joy
OH boy!
My Carmel "tigre" howls at the moon
and soon
in her climax
at its peak, in the max
she squirms shivers and squirts
In a puddle
we cuddle
Eyes rolled to the back of her head

Deep breaths
with no clue to what was done or said

I stroke my fiery feline's thigh
as she floats quietly into the sky

BAD TABBY

Driving to my house I held hands with this pretty lamb
Two steps into the door we passionately kissed
"Where have you been all my life?"
Was it something I missed?

On the sofa she introduced me to her Tabby
"Meow" she said, it wasn't too shabby
I kissed her tabby caressed it too,
And to my surprise the Tabby, real coy
expressed its joy
She served me a drink
to my surprise
"Nectar of the Gods!"
I cried.

The Tabby then climbed onto my bed
"Bad Tabby" I sad.
Run around the tabby did with no leash
A hand full of silk ties is how I tamed this beast
She purred on my sheets
even bolder.

Then she said,
Looking at my four post bed
"Tie me up! I want you!"
So silk ties came out
One red the other blue.

Even better
violently we loved
Screams and shouts no lesser
Claw marks on my back
Hand prints on her thighs
She shook with passion
As I came inside.

A WHILE BACK I WROTE

A while back I wrote
About a chest of treasure
And my future with it as I hoped
Full of fortune and pleasure

Then I came to see
That with it I was truly deceived
The treasure chest was actually
A cardboard box
Full of painted stones and rocks,
Plastic toys and what nots
Like a tourist in the New York City vortex
I purchased a fake Rolex
From a female who ran around
Like a greyhound in a playground

Mother of the year on Friday:
"I don't leave my daughter out after dark!"
Madame of the year on Saturday...
"Well she's fourteen and can stay and go…
At the convention center till 11 PM...
I've got company you know!
Well, he's just a friend"

You see,
From me,
You'll find sympathy
In the dictionary

Between syphilis
And s**t
And I'm so glad that the night of my birthday party
was when we called it quits

Discouraged and depressed
I was on Sunday for a minute
Several hours later I lined up dates
For Monday through Friday
And in the game
I was playing to win it

Then I met a young violinist
With the purest of hearts
With an angelic Celtic voice
Green blue eyes with ginger hair
With a sense of innocence

This French speaking violinist
Caused this Renaissance man's heart
To give in by choice
Withdraw from the game
Without a care to spare
To presently spend time
In her presence
Green blue eyes
And ginger hair
For now I truly appreciate
And love the treasure
I have that came from above

For (unlike you) she can cook
Is loyal
Has compassion
Honesty, and is truly a great mother
And in her modesty
A woman who knows how to love
And be a great lover
And to conclude this vicious rip
I asked you to get a glass of your Kinky drink
And stick your finger in it
Pull it out and see how the Kinky drink
quickly fills in the hole
Which is how fast I have replaced you
with another younger model
With better features as a whole.

Personified with a soul of gold.

MISTAKES

My dear Tabby,
Mistakes I've made
And I've made many
But being with you my dear,
Never had been one nor any
My love I cherished you from close and afar
In my bed, on my journeys and even in my car
Things I said accumulated in your mind
Rekindling bad thoughts from a previous time
The guy that did that should've never controlled
The fear deep inside that you hold
I love and honor thee
Please forgive me
For the things I've said
I didn't know at the times the infringements I had made
Don't set me free
Take a look inside my heart
I've destroyed it
Thinking and feeling of this depart
A broken heart is never given
Only earned…
And I've earned mines via Mistakes I've made,
And as I try to move on I'll learn.
This is the man you see before you now
Not the guy you had disallowed
Sorrow, tape and glue in hand

Mending his heart as best as he can

The last Renaissance Man

RESPONSE TO THE LETTER TO TABBY

Dear love of my life,

Last night was very tough.

I had to take an Ambien to sleep.

I missed you on my chest and my arms in my bed.

Your smell, your touch, your cute silly laugh, and your dry wittiness still linger in my heart with all of our cherished memories. But most of all, I miss the way you see the world with brand-new eyes.

I too am crying and choked up while writing this. The tears in my eyes make it hard to type on this stupid tiny text keyboard with my fat thumbs! Ughhh

I'll be celibate for the next months or until I know that cannot cause anyone any pain and I am healed. And I pray that you do the same and continue your journey of healing and strengthening to be able to love someone without any walls or equivocation in the future.

I figured it was too soon for you to have a relationship with someone, by the way you describe your previous ones. I was just wishing that we could've grown through all of this crap together as others had done before us. Forgive me for thinking so.

Can you please mark your calendar 1 month from now and reach out to me to let me know you're OK? Or at least keep me posted about your success in school via fb. I'm very proud of you and your accomplishments.

If you need anything (advise on car or apartment, etc.) please feel free to call or text me and ask, I will gladly give you the best advice I know as a friend and will keep it friendly and professional (I hate to see anyone be taken advantage of, like the Honda dealership tried). I'll help you with whatever way I can with no strings attached. You can trust that I am a man of my word, honor and good character.

Be strong my love, and thank you for giving me some of the best days of my existence. They will be cherished forever in my heart and never replaced.

I wish to see your beautiful face again someday and maybe we can rekindle what we had and move forward in a better condition than we are now.

And if not, I would still love to have your friendship and hear about your kids journey in life, because they're awesome kids with an incredible mother, who through tough times, with incredible strength and tenacity managed to keep them on the right course. And I'll be their best cheer leader!

Please don't forget to invite me to your graduation, for it would be my honor to attend, and I would be the loudest cheerer in the crowd for you.

If you haven't noticed, sometimes you shocked me into awe with your mental strength, wittiness, sage like overall knowledge and your ability to scrap up an incredible meal in seconds. I am truly a fan of yours and will continue to be so. So please, when you feel you are healed, I would love to see you face again, to just talk and catch up. Panera maybe?

There are a few poems I wrote that I would love to mail to you signed, so that you can place them in a box of memories. Can you please send me you address?

With all my heart and love
Valerio

LETTERS BETWEEN US

My dearest,

I made my mend with the Polished Princess yesterday. We spoke for hours at a restaurant, and I continuously apologized. She was really upset with the way I had treated her and is now actively in a great relationship with that guy I saw.

He treats her well and that's all that counts. She also said that she was proud of me for admitting my mistakes and taking ownership of the damaged I had done to her. With tears in her eyes and a lump in her throat, she forgave me and that's all that I needed. And I was humbly grateful.

We will both carry on separately in our lives at peace. And I wished her well.

Our breakup was my helicopter ride, and I am grateful to you for that.

I cry myself to sleep every night and wake up crying because to the wake of destruction I left behind in my life.

Please forgive me my love, for hurting you, as I've said before if I did. It was never intentional.

What I am hoping (in my healing process) to look you in the eyes and ask for your forgiveness. Whenever you feel you can see me.

And as I stated before, as time passes and we heal, maybe we can start over from scratch, and see where we go from there.

My heart belongs to you, and I will wait an eternity to be with you. But I need to know, if there is a glimmer of a chance of hope, that we can try again, to be together one day, and continue in life's journey, hand in hand, with the laughter we shared, and the smiles in our faces.

Is it possible for me to win back your heart? As your gifted drawing to me shows, will the couple on the mountains meet, and walk through the valley together. I pray they do.

I am not trying to manipulate you in anyway. I'm just trying to win you back. I just want to know if there is a chance for our love & romance to continue.

You can reply back with a simple yes or no and I will respect whatever choice you make.

But I'm willing to do anything... if you want to have a three-way Skype with your Doctor, I'll do it. Whatever I need to do to prove myself worthy of your trust and heart, I'll do it. And if you want me to go away, regrettably, I will do it too.

Take care my love,
Valerio

Valerio,
I am so glad that you have made your peace with Polished Princess. I hope she can find her way to a joyful existence. I hope you can continue to grow past the damage she did to you as well, and be whole apart from her. I know you will someday, because you are strong and you always accomplish what you set your mind to do. :0)

I don't want you to beg my forgiveness. I didn't break up with you because you hurt my feelings or did something mean to me. Those things can be worked out. I broke us up because we are not either of us ready for the intensity and commitment we had worked ourselves into. You have the demons and your past haunting you, and the compulsion to change the people around you. I have the practical reality of being in a massive stage of transition with school and a fresh divorce, and the emotional need for time and space and a slower paced relationship than you are comfortable with. Plus my great mental distraction of the kids and their own transitions and needs and issues. These things created so much stress between us, and were tearing us apart anyway.

When you ask me if we can have hope for the future, I cry, because I wish I could know that for sure. I think that I am completely giving up on pretending to know what the future may hold for me or anyone else.

I do know that neither of us will grow if we cling to each other, even the thought of each other. I think that to grow and have any chance of truly being past these things and stronger and healthier and able to make a wise relationship decision between the two of us, we have to walk away from each other and grow separately.

My very wise girlfriend told me that it is like holding a bird you want to keep. If you clutch it and squeeze it and cling to it, you will kill it. But if you open your hand, willing to watch it fly away, you are also giving it the chance to fly back to you. And you would rather see it soar and be vibrantly strong and beautiful, than see it crushed in your fist out of fear, even if it means you don't get to have it. By letting it fly, you are also giving it the chance to be yours, but from a place of strength and choice, not fear and desperation.

I think we have to open our hearts and let our relationship fly free. And we have to go about our lives as if we will never have it again, at peace with that reality, and finding joy and vibrancy and wholeness within ourselves, and wait to see if someday it returns to us. Clinging to each other, even in our hearts, will stop us from being able to move forward and become whole and happy without each other, which is the only way we could ever be whole and happy with each other.

So that is a hugely painful concept to put into action, but it is the path I am taking. I have opened my hand, told the universe that I do not want to crush this thing that I loved so much, and have released it to find its way. And I am going to move forward as if it was just a beautiful time that was given to me for a short while, cherishing the happiness that we had and the beauty we found. And I am going to let the world go on, see people and go places and raise my kids and take my classes and pay my bills. And I hope you will do the same.

I want you to date other beautiful women, I want you to go party on Overton Square with your friends and take Salsa lessons with your buddy, I want you to throw yourself into your job and kick a**, I want you to build your home into the nest you crave and throw crazy awesome parties and get better at corn-hole so those other beautiful women can't beat you. :0)

And I want you to remember me with your heart-fist opened to the sky, and free your heart from any fixation it has with me. Let it heal and grow and become strong. I think this is where you will struggle, Val. Not fixating on me. I think this will be the hardest and best point of growth you will achieve through all of this. Letting that fist open up and giving up something you want so much, so that it can heal and grow, and accepting that it may not come back, is the only way to ever have a chance of getting it back. And that goes against all of your protective, providing, eternally-loyal traits. Please, please try. Because I know for a fact that you will only crush the little bird that is our relationship, if you keep trying to net it and drag it back to you. It has to fly free. I want you to unfriend me on FB, because I don't want to be the one to do it. I think it has to be done, or we will only be delaying our ability to move on.

And maybe someday we will meet again, and you will have a

beautiful wife and I will have a handsome husband and we will just be sweet friends with happy memories that we share. Or maybe we will meet and we will both be single and ready to try to see if we can make something grow between us again. I don't know. I am not going to make that decision for us, because I just don't know. I just know what has to be right now, and that's why I am asking you to let me go.

 I am crying again and can barely see this screen, but I want to end this with telling you that these last two months have been amazing for me and taught me so much. I am safe in my little place over here, and I am going to be happy and have good times again, and I am going to be ok. Don't worry about me. I will not put myself in danger before calling you, I promise. Thank you for offering your help and protection and support to me and my kids. You are a very good man, and I don't take that for granted. I'm grateful knowing you are out there ready to come if I called for help.

 I am sending all the wishes in the world for happiness and peace for your heart.

Tabby

It is with deep sorrow, tears and regret, that I accept your wishes my love.

I have some poems to give you to keep in your memory box, to remember our past, my Bodies T-shirts that I promised you, and your toothbrush.

How do you want me to get them to you? Shall I mail them or drop them off at your door when you're gone?

You were truly the best thing that ever happened in my life, and whenever I see your hair clinging to my clothes, I pick it up and cherish it and place it by the picture you drew me. Your berets and clips, remain in the places you left them, untouched.

I hope that one day in the future we will meet, and become friends. I have changed my entire way of thinking about dating and relationships and now realize my folly. We gave into lust and our pleasures together because we were so starved for affection and emotion, and we were so naturally perfect together in all aspects.

I should have given you more time by yourself, to think, take care of the kids, get things done, take care of yourself and heal. For that I am sorry, and I know better now.

Adios querida.
Te amo muchisimo con todo de mi alma.
Mi corazon llora para ti.
Adios
Valerio

THE LETTER OF GOODBYES

Val,

I think we need to break things off. I am convinced that while we have awesome chemistry and enjoy each other's company and have had glorious moments together, there are deeper issues that mean our relationship will continue to struggle. I am not able to give the time and emotional energy to fixing a relationship right now, especially one that is only 2 months old. I believe that dealing with your feelings for The Polished Princess and your need to fix or improve me will best be done separate from a relationship with me. I also have my own growth to work on, and I can't grow and recover from my own many wounds while I am in such an intense and pressure-to-commit relationship. We both need to grow before we are able to give our hearts to someone else. It was just not meant to be for us. I cannot understand why these things happen and I am just starting to give up on trying to understand why.

I am heartbroken over this. I hope you hear that I have not made this decision lightly, or without much advice from people who know me best. I am crying as I type this, and I can't stand the thought of how you are going to feel as you read it. I need you to respect my decision and not try to talk me out of it. I don't want to meet in person, because I cannot stand the pain of it. Please don't try to see me. I am trying very hard to do the right thing, even when it hurts like hell. And this hurts like hell.

Please be good to yourself and keep moving forward. I am honored to have been with you, and loved by you, and brought so warmly into your massive circle of friends. You are a wonderful man and have every reason to look forward to a healthy and vibrant relationship that rocks your world someday. I will miss you.

With best wishes for all the good things in the world,
Tabby

NEVER IN MY LIFE HAVE I WOKEN UP CRYING

Never in my life have I woken up crying
And have fallen asleep crying
Drowning in my tears
Overcome by fear

Ashamed of the mass destruction I had left behind
All I can find are broken hearts
And body parts
That lay in my wake
As I run from this black drowning cloud
My soul it's trying to take-Right Now!

Small words properly place in a sentence
Leave a destructive result with no repentance
I'd placed them silently and strategically
Almost lyrically
Like a SEAL lying in wait
Detonator in hand
This bridge he'll take
As the masses cross across their fate
Grin on his face
Hit the button on the box!
Detonate!!

I can't breath
My chest paralyzed in thoughts
Here comes that cloud again
I'm gonna get caught!

Drowning in misery
Of my previous history
I have no peace
The destruction I've done
How can I sleep?

The thing I've said to her and my actions of selfishness
Overcomes my mind and willingness
To continue in the battle and clean up my mess
Memories of joy repeat miserly
Personify themselves entirely
Forgive my transgressions!

Weary now
Heart and soul with gaping wound
Fear abound-I'm consumed
I'm bleeding out
Grasping for air
I cough and shout
"Hear it comes!
The black cloud of despair"!
Consumed with Death
I gasp my last breath

Overtaking the horizon colorless
Surreal in black and gray
Refusing to go away

"Abandon all hope
Those that enter here"

I'm grasping my last rope
Palms on fire, it's all I can bare
I'm sliding down this bloody slope

It has taken plenty of souls
And none it'll spare!
Mines is next I'm told
And it hates to share.

Help me LORD
Please give me strength-My Lord
To exit this fight and be in your grace-My Lord
At your feet
Please let me be
Away from this hell I've created!
Mercy! Mercy!

Release me from this misery.

THE BEST 8 WEEKS OF MY LIFE (THUS SO FAR)

On an app to my amazement
I found a beautiful lady
Green eyes
With a copper crown
Possibly a schoolteacher or a librarian I thought
But actually a violinist, a tutor and a student
I messaged her on Friday
Saturday she responded
Sunday we met for coffee
Monday was a holiday and we met for sushi
The energy was intense we had to leave
"Box to go please"
Driving to my house this pretty lamb sat in my car
We held hands and I drove home
it wasn't too far
Several weeks had gone by
Every day better than the other
In her excitement she cried:
"I feel like it's our honeymoon every time we're together!"
"I love our life, it's almost a fantasy"
"I can see us together forever!"

These words echoed in my heart
As of today we're apart
Was it the Parties we had?
Friends we amused
Running around town
Being "edgy" and "fun"

Or was it just too soon?
She's in school,
Has a daughter, and sons
Saying that I must admit
No better lover or mother have I ever met
And to this day,
though my heart aches
I haven't an ounce of regret
No greater memories have I held
so close and dear to my heart
Thank you Lord!
I'm just sad I had her for a moment
Why did we have to part?

Fast forward to an intersection in time
When we meet again
Would she be willing?
For a second round?

Or just be my friend?
And leave it as we found?
With nothing to gain
Or resound.

THROUGH HER EYES

Through Her eyes
My life was colorless
Until now, this I recognize
Shades of gray and white
Darkness and light
No variance in sight
People who spoke of beautiful flowers and rainbows
How majestic the colors were
This I thought I knew
And sonnets and poems of it
I've written a slew
And if you asked me in true
Detail I would converse,
The shade of the color of the universe forward and reverse
Until one day I met her:
"A través de sus ojos vi
Lo ciego que estaba sin ti"
This copper crowned pearly skinned Aphrodite
Appeared to my delight
She spoke majestically of simple things of the heart
And through her eyes I saw its might
How she, majestically mixed it all
through her brilliance
As assimilated in her innocence
Life as it was supposed to be lived
Together in unison, not apart
Colors of the heart and song
The gift of love and loving

The gift of patients and waiting
Were the things she personified to me
And how I saw through her eyes
Thing never revealed to before.

"Y por eso le doy la gracias a mi amor"
Su amor y empresario
Valério

MY TABBY

My Tabby,
With Father Time I would plea,
To travel to your past
And remake your memories
I'd remove your bad history in times
And place happy future faces.
Mine.
So as you travel you can recognize
With no surprise
That I'm the one for thee
And you're the one for me

You see
I love every part of Thee,
From your head down to your toes
especially when you smile
and scrunch your nose
When you are nestled in my arms
Fully armored, no hurt or harm.
And when you feel as such,
Your eyes turn from green to blue
As a summers sky
Over the island of Lanai

Defined by your curly Crimson Crowne
Fully breast with rosy bosoms, so round
Soft lily esq skin
Pink pedal lips

Your intersection resembles
a pink rose with Scarlet vines
When I sniff it
my mouth salivates all of the time.

And like the Irish tenors
"I'll take you home again, Kathleen"
To where the grass is green
And the sun's rays beam
On a sea of forgotten dreams

Be we back in Greece,
As if I were Odysseus in The Odyssey
Your smile would launch 1000 ships
of suitors from Ithaca to claim your heart
Your tears would send 1 million more
into battle, impart
Your eyes are as green as the emerald Isles
A thought foreseen of 1 million smiles

Just like sand
Slipping through our hands,
So do the granules of time
Deceit our minds
And Here I stand
Trying not to fall
Pieced Heart in hand
Away from my walls
Mended as well as I can
Hoping like Lionel Richie,

That "Love will conquer all"

Be I, able to persuade
Father Time to compromise
To push through today
until that day we meet again
Or to rewind the hands of time
Thus to the day we met
A Sunday in May
With no regret
I'd unravel the thoughts that bind
So that our travel forward in time
Would not leave us afraid and blind

CHAPTER 4

Incipere (Inspire)

OUT OF THE ASHES

I had broken off all communication with Tabby, and was trying to keep to myself, working on myself. But Thanksgiving was around the corner, and I was feeling depressed again. So I hit the dating apps once more. I was on again and off again communicating with the Polished Princess and Tabby, with no avail. My heart was in pieces. And I was "looking" again. As the co-dependency bug was burrowing through my heart.

It was October, while scouring the dating apps, I saw this woman who peaked my interest. She was extremely pretty had a sarcastic tone on her profile. She had actually said some of the same things I said on my profile. We seemed like a good match, so I started texting her via the app. After a few days of back-and-forth texting and a little banter, I finally gained her confidence and she gave me her number. And we started texting back-and-forth via our cellphones, which led to several phone calls and hours of speaking on the phone. She was a young brunette in her mid-30s with a light red highlight on her hair (imagine that), chiseled chin, perfect white smile and teeth, and extremely intelligent. She was a certified critical care nurse working on her master's degree. She had a nice house in the right neighborhood, two teenage kids, a great head on her shoulders, frugal, witty as can be with a hint of sarcasm, sexy, in shape with an incredible body, and milky skin. She also had tattoos. Sixteen of them! Which blew my mind, because I had never dated girls with tattoos. Never! My paradigm was crushed and discarded. She enlighten me and open my mind to a different way of thinking and point of views. Nothing bad or out of the ordinary, but a lot of my self-induced prejudices disappeared with my paradigms. She became "The girl with the Phoenix tattoo."

She was a wide open book. We had good banter going on back-and-forth. She didn't take any of my crap, and wasn't hesitant to put me in check. I loved her personality and the way she carried herself with confidence and assurance. She looked and behaved great. She could get dressed up and go out on the town with me or hop on the back of my Harley and ride like a bad ass broad. There were times when I was an a** or said something stupid, and she would look at me and say, "Hon, (short for Honey) you need to rethink what you just said..."and she would call me out and point out that I did something she wasn't too fond of. A total one hundred and eighty degrees of the previous relationships I had had, where the women would let stuff fester and they'd make a list of things I said and did, that they didn't like. Only to explode afterwards, whipping out the list.

I loved that she called me out on my behavior, because that made me change and improve myself on the spot. There was no guessing or decoding what she felt. When she pointed something out to me and me to her, we would stop and discuss it on the spot, and squash it. Boom! No more issues. No list. Imagine that? We had incredible chemistry and were in sync.

She had just gotten divorced several months ago (yea, you'd think I'd learn by now), and was still feeling some emotional turmoil and pain from that divorce. She was married several times before and was very guarded about certain things. But yet, her charisma, beauty and charm keep luring me in. In one of our conversations she said, "You make me feel like a high school girl all over again. I can't wait to see you and touch you and smell you. I feel all giggly inside. Damn you!!! What have you done to my mind and my heart! I want you!!!"

She was perfect, but still something was wrong…with me.

Something I couldn't put my finger on.

Everything was going great. I had refinanced my house, I started to have money in the bank and I just finished remodeling the kitchen and the bathroom of the house, getting it ready for sale. And I had this dynamite woman by my side. It all was going as I planned, moving in a positive direction. But I felt incomplete and I didn't know why. It was as if I was waiting for a storm to happen. There was a giant quiet, an absence of noise all around me. It was all too perfect, and it scared me.

It scared me so much that I decided to go to church. I was going to meet God on his turf, instead of prostrate, face down on the living room floor. I decided to go to the local Life Church, not too far away from my house. My friends and acquaintances from my previous churches attended there and I figured it'd be a nice and friendly place to start all over again with people I know and trusted. But a funny thing happened to me on the way to Life Church. I drove right past it and continued down Germantown Parkway, and made a left on Walnut Grove Rd and drove towards Hope Presbyterian Church (Hope Church).

As I pulled in the parking lot, I didn't know what to do or where to go, so I just followed the masses inside. At the main entrance I saw a sign that said "singles group", so I walked into the venue and sat down. I looked around. I was curious about the dating pool, which didn't look too good at the time. I saw people (about 200 of them) that were happy being single and I thought to myself "what a bunch of losers! Who the heck wants to be happy single? I guess that's how you have to be if you're so messed up that you can't find someone else to want you."

Boy was I wrong! Here was another paradigm that was about to break.

At the singles group, this young pastor got up onstage.
A down to earth, charismatic African-American fella. And everything
he said was directly aimed at me.
Everything!
He might as well pulled me aside and have a talk with me and put
my name in the blanks of his sermon. His words were smacking me
on the fore head like, Biff hitting McFly (In Back to The Future).
The lesson that day was about Daniel. And the notes are worth
repeating in this book (with permission by ID Curry):

Hope Pres.
Singles class: Isaac Curry

Daniel 10:1 19-21
Lessons learned by Dan/ examples:
Chapter 9 = 2+2=4. Which is a simple answer.
*Chapter 10= (a+c) +[(5y x 127q- 6) 3.75] x8 = your mate. Which is a
complicated answer to a complicated equation.*
Don't expect a chapter 9 answer in chapter 10.
*Sometime we pray, pray, pray, for months or years, and don't receive an answer
so we quit and abort the download.*
He started to compare life to his computer activities, and hardships.
Don't abort the download, if you don't have the bandwidth.
If you abandon the download you won't receive the update.
*Sometimes the answer to your problem takes longer to get to you because it's a
struggle in the spiritual realm.*
*Your answer is in the delay. I was impatient, because I kept disrupting the
download process by getting into quick relationships. If you're not receiving the*

download, it could be because you're out of position. You're too far from the wireless modem. You need to get closer.

Maybe you have too many activities going on in your life. I couldn't download because I had too many windows opened on my laptop. In order to get the download, you need to close the programs running in the background.

We don't see the spiritual warfare going on in the background.

Chapter 9: A lower ranking angel fighting a lower ranking demon.

Chapter 10: A higher ranking Angel is fighting a higher ranking demon.

When praying you need to be looking.

Make sure you have the system requirements.

You need to know that you have the bandwidth (emotional stability, capacity, attitude, discipline) for the download.

After about 45 minutes of what seemed like a one way conversation with Pastor Isaac, him talking to me via the stage, the class was over. And in an odd (what the heck just happened to me) stupor, I followed the masses of thousands of people, to the main church.

Before I continue, let me tell you a little bit about me and main church. At the previous church I was a member of for 20 plus years, the house band took requests after the service. I had always ask those guys to play "stairway to heaven" by Led Zeppelin. And they refused to because it wasn't Godly enough (I suppose). Churches I had attended before were like cookie cutter churches. They didn't have a big mix of different nationalities, which was what I craved for, as part of my old Brooklyn, New York, melting pot roots.

So I walked into this church (Hope) and grabbed a seat somewhere in the middle. When I looked around, the crowd started filling in the seats. To the left of me were Asians, to the right African-Americans, in front of me were Spanish speaking people, and behind me, Indians and white folks. There was a giant mix of people in that church that day. It seemed as if every race and nationality in Memphis accumulated in the pews that morning, just for me. And they were all dressed in regular street clothes. No ties, suits or tux. And when the house band started playing, the first song they played for bumper music was...... "Stairway to heaven" by Led Zeppelin. They had me at "stairway to heaven!"

And I thought, "Ok God, I'm on your turf and you have my full attention now".

I can honestly say the worship music they played stirred my soul and detoxed my body via the tears in my eyes.
And when pastor Rufus (a black man) got on stage and started talking in his soft relaxed tone, and highly educated simple articulated speech (so that everyone can understand him), it was as if the Lord had put the exact words I needed to hear in that man's mouth, at that moment, to get me committed to Him. Rufus preached about Barnabas, and how weirdoes changed the world. He was talking one of the love language to my heart and soul. I felt cast out, like a weirdo, not knowing what to do or what direction to go with my life, and he was speaking to only me in that crowd of thousands.

When church was over, I really didn't want to leave. I hung around the main entrance people watching and absorbing everything that had just happened to me over the last two hours. It all was life changing, and I pretty much figured out, if I wanted to have a change in my life, I had to make a change in my life, now.
On the drive home I rededicated myself to serving the Lord. And

that meant that I had to give up my co-dependency with the girl with the Phoenix tattoo.

I fought it until mid-November, then gave in to what I had to do. We were getting into each other too deep. As I started attending Hope, and during my time in church, The Lord confirmed that there was a storm brewing in my life and I had to be prepared. I really didn't want to drag the girl with the Phoenix tattoo into my crap storm. I wanted to save her and protect her from what I was about to go through.

She was awesome and a bit fragile (at the same time) and I didn't want to be the "a**hat" that ruined her. I wanted her to have good memories of me, and maybe someday we could be friends or maybe more.

So with tears in my eyes and a stammer in my voice, I called her and told her that it was over.

Her response went something like this:

"What!?! You a**hole! I fell in love with you. I thought you said we were going to get through these tough months together?"

My reply:

"I know sweetheart, I'm very sorry, but I'm going to go through some stuff that I can't drag you into. This is my mess and I have to protect you from it. I'm very sorry. This is a walk in the desert that I have to do by myself".

And I had to! And I did.

What I didn't know then, I know now, and I know why.

I was incomplete, and so was she. We were co-dependent with each other. We couldn't move forward in life expecting someone else to fill in the holes of the missing spaces in our lives.

As Dr. Sid (askdrsid.com) puts it:

We needed to be two complete people independent of each other, satisfied with our selves, and happy by ourselves, with ourselves. And when two complete people come together, they complement each other independently. You shouldn't be looking for your better half. You need to have your better half intact, whole, and present it to the other person as a complete product".

And that was what I wasn't doing all along.

I was incomplete, trying to find someone to complete me, when in fact, I had to heal my wounds and complete myself, and present myself to the other person as a whole me.

Side note: Speaking of wholeness, after The Polished Princess had broken up with me a few months ago (we were on and off in between relationships). The last thing she told me was: " Oh Val. I'm just going to be alone. Be a single mom for now, working on myself... Blah blah blah...." Within days of spewing that crap, she reunited with her ex-boyfriend. The guy she was supposed to have broken up with, to be with me again.
I'm guessing she probably never broken up with that guy in the first place. I think she was using me as a filler while he was out of town. He was an upgraded version of her ex-husband. So I named her boyfriend "1.2" or Juan dot two. And I always referred to him as that to her, every time we talked or texted.
I was pissed, because she lied to me. And it started to fester. Most of the mad poems in this chapter are about her. Go figure.

November rolled around and Thanksgiving arrived. I'm a traditional guy and I enjoyed having Thanksgiving at my house with tons of food friends and family. I've done that all of my life. Instead I visited a friend's house with my ex-wife's niece (the girl I had raised since she was three). I usually picked her up from Franklin TN, on long weekends. The drive for me is exhausting. Sometimes I'd leave work at 3pm (I get up for work at 430am) and drive straight to Franklin, get her, then turn around and drive back to Memphis. Depending on traffic and how exhausted I was, it'd be a total of seven to eight hours on the road. Her mother stopped meeting me halfway for some reason or another which was why I had to drive both ways.

Both of my natural born kids had stopped communicating with me and had taken their mothers side. My oldest daughter was the heart and light to my life. She's used to call me every day and we'd talked for hours. She hadn't spoken to me in over a year. She was pregnant and I didn't know if I'd ever get to see her or the baby.

My son used to be my buddy. When he came back from war we'd sit in the living room, chat, laugh and just talk about "stuff". He's extremely comical and charismatic. He has this funny laugh that when he starts laughing, you have to laugh too! Within seconds the whole house starts to laugh and stuff and drinks start to squirt out of peoples noses... he's hysterical!

When he found out about the divorce and the affair he cut off all communications with me except when he'd text me to curse me out, because his mother was sad or mad about something. I didn't know why nor did I care why. The real problem here was that he totally disrespected me every time I would try to reach out and talk to him. So I told him, "Son, respect will not cost you a dime, but disrespect will cost you everything."

After he told me to f**k off a few times, I repossessed the truck that I had bought him so that he may attend and finish college in middle Tennessee. It was under my name, I was paying the note and the insurance for it. So legally it was mine. Would you lend your truck to someone who totally disrespected and treated you like crap? No, right? I didn't think so.

I used to feel like it was my fault. I had never set any hard boundaries with them. And when I tried my ex would push back on them. So now when I tried set a hard boundary, they didn't like it, and shut me out.

Oh well, that's their choice and their lost.

As the month of December started, and loneliness haunted and taunted me, my feelings for "the girl with the Phoenix tattoo" still lingered hard. A hundred times I wanted to call her and hear her soothing voice saying my name and calling me "Hon". I was a total emotional mess and a hurting unit.

In addition to the loneliness, my step dad (Jose), wanted me to give him four thousand dollars, so that he can pay a Santera (a voodoo witch doctor) to remove the bad spirits from his house that were crippling him. She was running a scam on him and had taken a bunch of money I'd left him as emergency money. He didn't like my reply of "no". So he too ex-communicated me. I used to call him every other day. He was like my adult child and now he too wanted nothing to do with me.

I'm his caregiver, he lives in Puerto Rico and I live in Memphis. Communication is vital, when you're trying to take care of an 86-year-old man that has severe arthritis on his knees and hips that lives by himself in the Caribbean, in a cement house on stilts.

Every Time I'd called him, he'd say in Spanish, "I'm not dead yet!" And hang up.

What the hell!!!

See a problem here?

I thought so.

To top it all off my natural dad (Anel) passed away in Puerto Rico. And a last minute airline tickets out of Memphis was one thousand eight hundred dollars. Ouch!!!
I was facing the eye of the storm dead on while in flight to Puerto Rico.
I thank God for the black lady sitting beside me on the plain. She had an entire pack of tissues to give me, as well as a warm heart, soft hands to hold mine, and a listening ear. Thank you whoever you were. Your warm spirit helped me get through that part of my journey. And I am grateful that you came along. May God bless you indeed.
Now in Puerto Rico, me, my step brother (Jr) and step sisters (Lisa and Maria) had to rally around my step mom (Nelly) and the family. We all performed as a unit. When one was down, the others were up. We never left Nelly alone for any extended time. It was a very tough time for all of us, especially me, the oldest. I had to be cool, calm and loving to my family while suppressing the s**t storm I was in. My dad (Anel) was supposed to live forever. He was one of the younger ones of his peers.
What the heck Lord!
What the heck!!!

Can you see why I hate December?

Oh, how I wish I could have taken "The Girl with the Phoenix Tattoo" with me or at least be able to call her, and speak to her, so that she could sooth my hurt and tell me everything was going to be alright. But now, I had to rely on God to help me. This was the third December in a row that tragedy had taken its toll on me. I was exhausted physically, emotionally and spiritually. I had no more to give. The migraines came back with avenges. I wanted to die with my father (Anel) and be buried besides him. But I had to stay strong and take care of my step dad (Jose-even though he didn't want to speak to me), and be his rock, as everything around me seemed to crumble and was set on fire. My step father (Jose) loved my biological father (Anel-they were brother in laws). They were like brothers and they had an exciting history. He took it hard. Two years ago Jose's wife (Natividad-the matriarch of the family) my adoptive mom (and biological aunt) had passed away at the age of eighty four. (I wrote a poem about her in chapter 1). She was my rock and the light of my life. And now I had to pay it forward. In full, and on demand, to Jose, and the rest of the family.

And so, I took another painful step forward to continue the journey, one step at a time, and one day at a time.

Here is my struggle in poetry form.

OCTOBER 23 - PICASSO

I'd like to say
I have discovered
A Picasso like no other
Born and bred on the same day
94 years apart but who's to say
Had Pablo lived another two
And have seen the birth, anew

Seeing of her beauty he would've brewed A Muse
Of a scarlet crowned dame
Wild as the untamed flame
"La beauté de cuivre" would've been her name
Compiled of smiles in a cubist fashion
Curvy hips flaming mane
Full of passion

Would he had added her to "es demoiselles d'avignon"
Full figured bust exposed
With other women in the salon

Would she had been the figure in "la reve"
A beauty sleeping in a crimson chair
Eyes shut, hands on lap
Without a care

Had he seen us together and portrayed us in "The kiss"
A couple embraced
Completely in bliss

I Reminisce
We kissed A few times like this

Now forward to October of the year 2015
When at a particular place
The Renaissance Man meets the Polished Princess
To talk future business
About a future unseen
Will the Princess become his Queen?

Will it be like Delta Dawn
Memory of days long gone
In a book of poems and song?

Or of future chapters
Of the years after?

Strolling in the surreal sunset
Memories they will never forget

From there on after

Letter to PP

For the past few months, I have gone to bed crying, and have woken up crying… Sometimes unable to sleep, I have to take half of an Ambien.

Last night and this morning was no exception.

And I am actually pushing back the tears and sadness of all the pain I have caused as I write this.

Thank you for sharing with me your pain and for giving us closure. Enclosed is the poem I promised you.

Take care my sweet,

Val.
(RM)

Her reply:

It's beautiful. You were truly inspired. I'll cherish this and all the others I have received over the past two years; each one has moved me emotionally.

Valerio, I want you to be the man I know you can be - the one I got a glimpse of last night as you patiently listened to and acknowledged my feelings. You showed me more respect last night than you ever have before… I deserve that and appreciate that more than you know. It's the small things that mean so much… I have no bitterness towards you and I finally feel at peace. It was so important to me that I vent and resolve my anger towards you or I would have carried that around far too long and been on a horrible path. You gave me that chance like a real, honest man with the courage to face the harsh words I had to say and listen and apologize. I truly forgive you and it feels so peaceful.

A la prochaine fois

(RH/Polished Princess)

MY LITTLE HUMMINGBIRD (TABBY)

I came across a Selasphorus Calliope
Wounded on a grassy slope
Beauteous as she was

Copper crowned and teal scarfed
Delicate in her presence
In a state of topor

I scooped her up gently,
Held her in my hand
And admired her beauty and delicate stand

Home with me
Was where I wanted her to be
I'd feed her, take care of her
Protect her from all predators

But I couldn't, you see
For her majesty was in her flight of freedom
Not in my captivity

So I remove some twine from her wings
The only thing stopping her from flight
I then let her free to her delight

Hard as it was to let her go
She captured my heart, I'd tell you so

For if I didn't she'd surely die
For she was meant to be free

To hum and fly

AS I WALK AROUND MY HOME

As I walk around my home
I find strands of her red curly hair along
on the carpet
my shirts and suits in the closet

And to my amazement
I pick them up
Roll them in a ball
And place them on my cigar box on my dresser draw
next to the picture she drew before
My heart swells up and the tears seep, On my expensive shirts
That I now value as cheap
Of all the bounty in my possession
That strand of hair is what I value and cherish the most

As we traveled through the maze of life
With perfect timing on her side and mines
As if guided by a greater Hand
We found ourselves together
Face to face
smile to smile
There at this intersection of life she opened up to me and I to her
we love passionately
and we intertwined incredibly

at this intersection we met for just a brief moment
Fork in the road before us
I asked her to travel with me

To the destination I seek
and she decided to take
the other side and travel alone
One day in the future I hope we meet
And continue together
In this strand of time
and continue conquer the maze of life

CHIMES

Chime, chime chime
Every time time time
Another text text text
It drains my power power power
On the hour, hour hour
Now ring ring ring
My cell I cling cling cling

The angel of death is texting and calling
I must not answer my phone
In my dreams we're talking
inside a garden of stone
His face is blank but his eyes are crystal-clear
As he stares inside my soul
He converses about my fears
"You're lonely and I see how heavy are your tears"
Don't you know that no one is suffering in here?"
"Yes my garden of stone is full of bones
of people from years gone past
So take my hand
and follow my path
You know as well,
this life was not meant to last"
"Give up!
Your sorrow is deep!
Take my hand and with my sickle I'll put you to sleep"
"Why would they care when your bones touch the ground?"
"Do you think they'll bring flowers?

Do you think they'll come around?
Open your eyes and wake!
So we can make this dream for real!"
A cold sweat
I wake and his presence I still feel.
My mind is clouded
I know not what's fake nor real
My thoughts are jumbled
The previous happy memories he did steal.
As I lumber, trying to slumber again again and again
His voice echoes in my ear, "Don't forget me my friend.....
my friend........friend."

HEY GIRL...

Hey girl, it's me again
what's this game you're playing?
With all those little boys dressed like men
Even though I was one
I'm no longer like them

I go around trying to love
with my heart on my sleeve
Trying to love on the women I meet
and mend their broken dreams
Discarded women destroyed by careless boys
Who tossed them aside like broken toys

Your perfume hides your arrogance
But It can't hide your emptiness
While you go around baby
with no heart to share
you reel men in baby
with a smile and a toss of your hair
Playing your game with broken boys
Who carry little toys

Yeah I've seen their cars is in your driveway
You standing sideways
trying to act so coy
Batting your eye at those broken boys
In your robe kissing them goodbye

Time after time, guy after guy
You have the neighborhood talking baby
about the crazy redhead in the cove
"They're stopping buy her house,
in droves...
Who's the guy she's with this week?
She kissed him on the cheek...
The one in the Infinity
There are two you know...
Is it the silver one or is it gold?"

They say opposites attract
but you know we're same
I play with broken hearts
You play your crazy games

But there's a difference baby
The one that sets us far apart
When it comes to broken hearts
You play with the pieces baby
and abandon them at their doors
I mend the pieces baby
and try to leave them better than before

Yes you're hot and sassy
and your vanity has the best of you
But I don't think you're that classy
Because I see right through you
You're a broken girl baby
Incomplete as can be

Because the pieces you're missing baby
Are shaped like me

Remmy

Aka: Glaoco from Yaoco.

CHECK MATE

That's a nice game of chess we played the other night
No witnesses nor mess in site
A few beers and some wine
I saw you lined up your pieces from left to right
Dressed to the nines
Hoping that I'd bite

Victory is the song you played
during the day and through the night.
But the lyrics you sang
kind of gave you away.

I'm standing behind my castle now
Safe and sound
while my knights overlook the pawns
You played around town.

It's not the first time I've played this game of yours
For goodness sake
The last time we played
It ended in stalemate

Now my moves flow silent and swiftly
like a submarine
I took your Bishop
Now I'm after your King

You beat me with a "Fools Mate"
The first time around
and I'm leery of your moves you make
Prancing around town

The clock is ticking baby
You're running out of time
It's time for your retreat- lately
Your hearts sublime

You're running out of pieces maybe
You're going to be beat
It seems like your pawns
are adding to your defeat

I know this game isn't for you,
because you "Have too many things to do".
You're looking kind of bored- lately
uncertain how to score

I know you want romance baby
But you're playing the wrong board -badly
with the wrong pieces by you side
It's your turn to move….

What will you decide?

THE ONE THAT GOT AWAY

There isn't anyone that can read your mind like I can
No woman child or man
There isn't anyone that knows how you feel like I do
Girl I know everything about you
Nobody can love you and fill you with pleasure
Girl, because I'm your treasure
When you put your head on my chest and you fall asleep
You slumber heavenly, really deep
When I rub your thigh and your back
you're always at peace to take a nap
When I write my songs and poems
And my dreams take us around the world
and leave us in Rome
Your heart gets enlightened
And your girly parts get excited

I know....

Because it all starts to flow
That's when you smile
And that little corner of your lip turns up for a while
Then your nose starts to crinkle
Your eyebrows wrinkle
Your eyes focus on every detail of my face
Doesn't matter who's around our space
Your fingers twirl the dark curls in my hair
Passer byers stare, but you don't care
You want to love me right here, or there

It's me that you're focused on
Your heart starts singing our song
Our bodies embrace in a dance, when I turn on the romance
I flip every switch in your mind and heart

That's what'll set me apart....

From all the guys that'll come after me
You'll see.....
You'll look back at our history
And the nights that led to these great memories.
Whether it's tomorrow or today
I'll always be the one.....

.... That got away.

OH MY POLISH PRINCESS

Oh my Polished Princess
What have we done?
In a frenzy
To be in each other's arms as one
In the midst of chaos
We've set off multiple lights and alarms
We've painted this town
From the Alchemy to the Zebra lounge
From garages to parks
And parking lots
Behind museums and churches
Our love and lust prevailed
And entailed us to continue
This fantastic tale
Laughter, tears,
Misunderstanding
To understanding
The misunderstanding
Any average pair
Would've never been left standing
Demanding their hearts
to sit still and silent-commanding

During a perfect affair
We should've been fair
And put aside our cares
And Ended it right there

You see from the beginning
We were doomed
When you spoke about that day
Alone-in your retirement room
With your memories loom
You'd look back at *our history*
Repeatedly revealing revelations
About our perfect romance

Wondering, the ending of...

His story.

AND THE CURVY REDHEAD HAD HER SWANKY WAYS

And the curvy redhead had her swanky ways.

With a flip of her hair, hand on her hip and the batt of her emerald eyes,

a table reserved for some fair haired couple was quickly given to her and her date.

A prime spot in the middle of the restaurant where all eyes can glaze and adore her presence.

Her copper hair naturally straight, was persuaded to curl down her back.

Her form fitting Versace red dress fell short three inches above her knees.

Her French manicured hands contrasted perfectly with her matching Prada "Tessuto e Saffiano" framed clutch. Her Red satin Prada platform pumps enhanced her over-the-top confidence and made the host gasp when he surveyed her from top to bottom.

With a two-tone Rolex on her wrist and cannery diamond ring dripping down her hand, no one would've ever thought that this woman working the room had ever worked all her life.

But would've imagined that she was a revered woman of leisure and pleasure. Hedonistic, perhaps.

Pampered by the tanned and toned curly, black haired Latin man that paraded beside her.

The royalty of Lucy and Ricky was reincarnated on this night, causing a stir.

The elegance of this Renaissance couple set the room a blazed. And the audience adored them.

Spotlights of whispers followed them to their table and subsided when they sat. Then they all gazed.

At the table the maître d' and his subordinates awaited their presence. His trumpeted greeting and courteous bow were skewed by his Spanish accent.

Contrary to the suggested seating arrangement, they sat beside each other touching knee to knee.

Her hand grasping his strong manicured fingers and squeezing them tightly.

When asked what to drink, her date responded in perfect Castilian Spanish,

"Para ahora, aqua, porfavor... Y si puedes, dejanos queto para un momento, porfavor".

Her huge Emerald eyes changed to Safire, as she tunneled through him, and smiled, crinkling her nose, as she squirmed on the polished leather seat.

He knew that speaking Spanish would set the fiery feline off, and moisten her tiny undergarments.

WRETCHED CUPID

Oh little wretched Cupid
How these lovers hold you high
I exclaim they're stupid!
That I cannot deny!

A bounty on thy head I doth have
3000 crowns and more I'd pay,
And I'd be glad
500 for thy bow
500 for thy quiver
2000 for thy head
I would gladly deliver!

What a total disgrace
You've made of my heart
Thy arrows Pierce
Hitting smart on the mark
With thy wicked laughter
And sarcastic banter
Don't you see my sorrow?
In my today's and tomorrow
And thee misery
That you have brought to me in this rant-er
You playful winged eunuch
With your mangled harped music
I'd drain thy blood in my decanter

Thy jaded spaded ruby arrow

Pierced sharply in my vessel
I tried to pull it out,
With it I wrestled
Nestled in my veins
That supersedes my brain
Thy arrows venom drives me
Truly insane
And low becomes my will
With lost control of my won't
I wrestle my emotions
Ye control of my "don'ts"

Oh thy wretched dickless little man
How I'd tear you apart
With both of my hands!
And carve your chest like art

Oh how I pray
On the day of Valentines
Medusas face
You would see
In perfect irony!

I'd gather thee
And place thee
By a rotted tree
Where four-legged friends
And fowls alike
Would foul your corpse
To my delight

And In the morning I'd awake
And foul thee again
With my bodily breaks.....

....And in my relief
I'd depart with a grin.

I'M NOT THE SAME MAN

Like a wilting rose in a dry vase
I have no apace
My youth is gone
But my thorns linger sharp
Like an abstract Arp
I'm a broken vessel
Empty inside
Although I smile
This I cannot hide
I am naked and ashamed
Before you my Lord
Running from my consequences
That which I abhor
Like a forgotten flower
Trampled on the ground
I'm not the same man
That used to be around

Written while at Hope Church

THE ARROWS OF YOUR CRITICISM

The arrows of your criticism
Pierce my body and drain my life
But I will remove it with my knife
Bandage it, and carry on through the night

Your gestures are like stones cast upon on my feet
Pulling me down into the sea's deep
But my creed is deeper
And I shall not surrender to the reaper

Your sarcastic whispers
Buzz around my ears
Like mosquitos
But I will ignore it
And not feed your ego

Your eerie looks tear into my flesh
Like a horseflies bite
Motionless I won't thresh
And give you that delight

Your presence casts a shadow
Upon my soul
But I will not give up
But shake off the cold
And drink stew
From my heated cup

Your hate is that of Diocletian
Like Saint Sebastian
I will not deny my love
Bound to the tree of your lies
Pierced like a sea urchin
My love will be the balloon
Of my ascension
In flight
Like a dove with no ties

This I hold certain

(Based on the story and my print of St. Sabastian, by Frank Martinez Andujar)

MEMPHIS TENNESSEE

Memphis
Ah city on the bluff
I can never get enough
Of your partying soul
With its music so bold
Blues and Motown on Beale
Rock n roll in Huey's, makes it all real
Rayford's and its disco
They have a dance pole you know
And so much more music, as the mix goes

From Alchemy to the Zebra lounge
The best piano bar I swear
You will find great places to hang
Without a care

Downtown, Midtown, the Island of Mud,
Is where it all happens, I can never get enough
FedEx forum its blood is blue
Full of Grizzlies and Tigers- I'm telling you
The Fans of the teams are second to none
They're loyal 'till the end, even on dry runs

Overton Square is growing leaps and bounds
That's where I hang, you'll always see me around
Cooper & Young so colorful its streets
With rainbow flags displayed at places we eat
Let's cover the suburbs and here's the mix

Bartlett and Cordova are the blue collar fix
Collierville and Germantown home some celebrity chicks

Our healthcare consist of best of the brew
LA Bonner, Baptist, and Methodist too
VA, the Med, and lovely St Jude
And a bunch of specialty clinics just to name a few

We might not have what other cities boost
And that's what I love about my city the most

Memphis is the smallest big city
You'll ever live in
We all are one family
We welcome you friend.

UNCLE SUGAR

Those who want not take not
But Uncle Sugar taketh away
Taking from the anorexic
To give to the bloated diabetic
Uncle sugar puts the working class
On a low sugar diet
And tells the working class
To be quiet
And feed the non-working class
With amenities on what the working class need
With both sides being disquiet
One that was taken from
The other that it was taken to
For how can we stand anymore?

How has this stood the test of time?
What's yours is mine
And what's mine is mine
It's the philosophy of this crime
That bounds us to these ill minded parties
Who in their fatten diet
Feast on the minds of the weak
And devour the strong to become meek

...acting like carnies.

HAVE I EVER TOLD YE HOW MUCH I ADORE THEE

Have I ever told ye how much I adore thee
Like the butterfly carefully grooming the flower
I adore thee
My heart is over whelmed
Every hour
Like a bee in a field of wildflowers
Thine presence is my heaven

Like a young mother holding her first born
My labor pains of life vanquish
When I see thee
And when I see ye
Slumbering smile
In the morning
And I touch ye skin
My heart becomes overjoyed
As such
For raw love is protruding within
And I remember not
What life was without thee
Nor can I fathom how to continue
Without thee

I feel so blessed
Listening to thy slumbered breath
It crescendos like the waves on a desolate beach
Within my reach

Thou's persona is as refreshing
As the first morning air of spring
My heart sings
Like the robin
At first light
Thy art the moon to my nights
Like the rain to my desert
Thy love averts my suffering
Thou art thee air to my wings
Thou art thee water to my springs
Thou art thee alto to my Opera

...and thee light to my candelabra

(Inspired by Corals baby boy, Rafael, on the first day of fall)

ELEPHANTS IN THE ROOM

Elephants in the room
Linger in your mind
The kind I cannot see nor find
About a sour past and things unsaid
They echo loudly in your head.
They control our future,
But lay in the past
A dark shadow they cast

One that is named inaccurate assumptions
He's feed by the false presumptions
That removes the gumption
Of love's resumption

The other is led by outdated information
Like the Thracian
Is the causation
Of loves dilation
Leaving your heart with a numb sensation
Entangle in expectations
Never defined
On either side

The other pachyderm
The emotional storm
Which takes dorm
In the form
Of Buried anger

Whom like a cancer
Takes anchor
Removes all cantor
And roots itself as a poisons tree
Whose fruit would be
Hate and resentment
When eaten destroys our sentiment
Creates a bitter temperament
And postpones the delicate betterment
Of our love

So to all that read this
A truth that we cannot miss
For love to exist
We must not cower
But take power
In inquiry
And not be wary
Of asking questions
Of things mentioned
To relive the tensions
For a love to bloom

We must learn to dance
With the elephants in our room
And lead them out the door.....
To their doom.

Inspired at Hope Pres, Based on singles sermon

GIRL WITH A PHOENIX TATTOO

I met a girl with a Phoenix tattoo
Along with fifteen others, I'd tell you
Skin truly smooth and white
An amazing canvas
An artist delight
Additive to touch
Yes-she's gifted
Drowning pool blue eye
Tough girl appearance
On the outside
Victim to no one's chide
Tender passionate sensual inside
Laser focused she can
"I get what I want. Even my man"
Outgoing smart ass sarcastic
Whose personality is mastic
And she'll take you on a fantastic
Ride to the other side
Of pleasures never known
With screams and moans
That would awaken
The common stones
In a delightful bare field I was shown
For she was endowed
And made me bow
To an unspoken passion
That lived inside
Neither man nor woman can deny

With a soothing kiss
A little chit and chat
We lead to this and that
Encouraging and
Endearing as she is
She personified
What it is to live

And the day
Gave way to night
As we were consumed
In our delight
And from today through the day I die
She'll be remembered and immortalized
As the girl that stepped into...
My life.

As the girl with the Phoenix tattoo.

WE HAD TEXTED SEVERAL TIMES

We had texted several times and set the date for Saturday. This being Thursday, two days seemed as if it would be two centuries to meet the raspy voice. We spoke on the phone and agreed to meet later tonight at eight thirty, in the local blue collar bar and grill, on the patio. I received a text from her when she got to the parking lot, "I'm here Hon. Where are you?"

"In the patio, far corner, see me waving? I'm the guy in the Barney suit, with the balloons." I texted back.

Through the plate glass window I could see her short dyed red hair, full figured body strutting through the opened door. Shawn the bouncer, opened the second door for her and surveyed her top to bottom, then back up again, with a grin on his face. His blue eyes followed her to the right as she waved back to me. He saw me waving back from afar, and gave me "the nod" of approval. The one that guys code each other, acknowledging the "score."

As she walked out the patio I can see her slanted smile smirking.

She wore a cream colored camisole shirt with silk spaghetti straps that were at their limit, restraining in place, her prominent breasts, as it draped down to her waist. Over that, she worn a thin tan sweater, which matched her worn tan cowgirl boots with turquoise stitching. To end the ensemble, she styled black form fitting leggings that outline her curvaceously full body, beautifully bringing it all together into a perfect package, with no panty lines.

She then came to the bench seat and we sat facing each other. At that point I touched her hands and smiled saying, "Hi. Come here, I know what you want". I then leaned forward slowly and caressed her face with my right hand, running my fingers through her hair while moving further forward kissing her on the lips. I could feel the electricity melt us together. In an instinct two strangers suddenly became one.

She purposely passionately kissed forward, then slightly pulled back, saying: "woo, that's a first for me on a first date".

In which I replied, "This is a meet and great babe, I can't wait to see what happens on the first date."

We held hands, ordered two beers apiece and spoke for what seemed a Nano second. My watch lied to me and told me it was an hour and a half later. We set the first date for Friday at three in the afternoon instead of Saturday. As I walked her to her car and opened her door, our lips merged as once again to say good bye. This time I ran my right hand up the curved small of her back, then downward to her butt cheeks, sending her to an instant moan. "Well. Then I'll see you tomorrow, Hon". She softly said.

"Sure sweetheart, I can't wait", I whispered, holding back my excitement.

Friday came and I left work early. We had texted most of the day and we had each other primed. I brought her home and as we took two steps into the door we began to embrace and kiss. Ten minutes later I was disrobing her in my room. As her clothes fell off, I can see the ink throughout her body contrasting her pearly tight skin.

Her tattoos were beautify shocking.

I had never been with a women who had so much ink on her-if any at all.

My boundaries and paradigms were heaved open like a crypt, and the stench of what was, got sucked out into the air, like the popping of a Coke can.

Her ink read like a register of events in her life's tale. Whereas the common woman would put ink to paper and record their narrative of pain, hardship and accomplishment in a flowery book with a locket, and a hidden key to enshroud a book of mysteries inside a hidden shoebox, tucked away in an obscure corner, under a pile of old clothes in the bedroom closet, this atypical fem didn't. She used the tribal approach of mapping life's triumphs and hardships. True beauty personified on her body for an exclusive few to see and read. The ancient method of which had been passed down through indigenous generations since the beginning of mankind, to memorialized all war weary warriors bloody battles of victory, pain, substantial suffering, and scars on their bodies. This petite Amazon was no exception.

Her body boldly detailed her life's journey.
A battle with Cancer, and surviving the feat marked her left shoulder high and proud. A ribbon with green butterfly wings and a dreamcatcher with blue feathers. "It holds good dreams. It's my dream to remain cancer free, Hon..."
Kanji Letters down her back: "My mistake tattoo. They mean forever happiness in marriage". That which she longed for disappointingly several times.
A medical symbol midst of her back, her triumph of being a critical care certified nurse, so that she may repay the kindness given to her in her fight.
Another Kanji symbol of mom on her overly sized luscious left breast, viewable, just above the bra line, indicated that this lioness has cubs.
On her right shoulder a Mandala. Tibetan dot work flower from the top of the shoulder halfway down her triceps. That of Art and beauty she treasures, which balances her shoulders. On the right side of her rib cage floats The Phoenix tattoo. Filled in blue ink, "Out of the fire rose a beautiful bird with powers stronger and

better than it was before". Thus far, the biggest tattoo on her body, marking her biggest struggle to victory.

Don't we all bare a Phoenix in our lives?

Through all of this ink, sarcasm and all around tough girl stanza, no one could see the young girl who played the viola, and had gained scholarships to various universities using the delicate instrument as her vehicle. Or a single mother of two children living in suburbia in a planned development, a soccer mom pursuing her Master's degree, setting the example to her cubs, raising and watching over them with the love compassion of a lioness. Nor would they see the beauty that lied within, a full robust women with passion, heart, an erotic sense of playfulness that few men can tame.

And when she surrenders her flesh to the male willingly, there is no greater euphoric rage that the average man can withstand or keep composed, than that what she's unleashed onto me.

She was truly an open book that remained a mystery. Too many riddles and unanswered questions aired around her. Dots and dashes that needed decoding. Small delicate locked boxes that needed to be opened.

And she kept drawing me in.

CHAPTER NINE

LETTER TO PP

Dear beloved,

I hope when this letter reaches you that you're in a better place than when we parted.

I also hope that your family situation has resolved itself and you are free from any drama caused by the crazies in your life.

During my time away from you I've brought into light in my mind several words we've exchanged in the past. And I wish that I can take them all back and say what I meant properly to you. But time rewinds for no man.

I've also come through early realization that if this relationship where to move forward we would need to leave behind all the extra luggage and only carry with us "what fits in the overhead compartment or the seat in front of you". :)

Of our relationship I mostly remember the good times and the smiles on your face, the joy and love we shared. But when we speak, mostly what you remember and talk about are the bad times and the BS we went through during the infancy of our relationship. That's why my doctor said that we needed space and time. So that you can drop and leave that luggage behind. And hopefully you will no longer hold that against me in the future and we may be able to continue new again as lovers or friends.

It was amazing to me how I sat with you in the hospital on Sunday, took you to the Janet Jackson concert on Tuesday, we made love on Wednesday and Thursday I knew you wanted to break up again. Again a misunderstanding on my words and the way you personified your previous relationship to me. You see I thought you were bragging on that guy and that flipped a quick switch in my head saying "then why the hell are you with me..." And as you know the rest is history. My deepest apologies.

I just want you to know that even though I cannot be "that guy", I can be who I am, giving you the same attention and love you desire, if not much better. Together we share an amazing chemistry. And as I meet new and different people, I see that our chemistry is tough to duplicate and a point that I will not compromise, because of my previous prolonged mechanical relationship with my ex-spouse.

I hope to one day reconnect and see you again, and if we both are in the right place and frame of mind, maybe we can start again, with a clean slate and no previous hard feeling.

Adios mi amor, y felize compleaño. Que lo pase bien.

Yours truly

The Renaissance Man /Remmy

AS THE TEARS RELEASE MY SADNESS

As The tears release my sadness
Through my eyes
Burned my face
For this I sigh
And I, sadden and feeling of disgrace.

I have to report
In short
That the love story of the Redhead
And the Renaissance man
Has come to an end
Never meeting on Picasso's birthday
A week before then
He had been with her
And her mind was set

At peace
I have always been.
I'm just incomplete
I am a complex puzzle
Missing one piece
And it's shaped like you
I was hoping we could reconcile
Start brand-new
We really never gave it a true effort
I'm sorry that you feel this way
My heart will never be the same
An amazing team

Together we dreamed

She: I'm sorry, too much past stuff.
I know it won't work it's just too much....
And we are just getting older
So best to move forward
And progress...
So I know this to be the very best..."

I am sorry that our past
Got in the way
Of a fulfilling bright future
Of sunny days
You're my first true love
Will always be
After all the fog cleared
I could see
Yes-I faced father time
With no fear
Thinking and concluding
Of how our love was dear
And how life
Has nothing to offer
Without you
There was no proffer
If only you'd let it go
And let me show
How true I really am
And that I am the man
You have always wanted

As your previous letters has said

I think that it is crazy
That you're trying to find
In a fog so hazy
What we had all the time
Together exclusively
With each other conclusively.
With another?
"I'm willing to forget, if you are..."
And from afar she answered:
"Just let me be...
I have to be alone now.
It's as far as I can see..."
With a sorrowed brow
I replied to the ring of her bell...
"Very well".
Maybe sometime in the future
Our paths will cross again.
And we won't have to feign.

"Shakespeare could've never written
In a days or midnight hours
Such a sadder
Ending to a love story than ours...
Nor a tragedy..."

She responded: "Agree"

So now this love that we had lit

I've learned to let it go.
I no longer have a candle lit
By my window.

"Adios mi amour".
Your one and only,
Renaissance man
Remmy

I AM IN SEARCH TO FIND.

I am in a search to find
Where's this nemesis of mine?
Revolving, evading me expeditiously
Exploiting my weaknesses
Estimating my underestimates
Exposing my evasions
He's an unpredictable predator
Persistently plotting the place
Of my downfall and disgrace

Like a consistent count
Continuously counting
My stumbling steps
As I fail falling forward to my folly
Be he Murphy or Motisi,
A master of self-modification
Who masterminds my mistakes
Am I the unfortunate Fortunato?
Being led through the palazzo
Silently stepping on the terrazzo
Through the catacombs of my mind

As I gazed in the mirror
I felt a chill, no a terror!
Of the shadow of the bearer
Who plotted my errors - even more
And to his frivolous fortune
He seems quite happily handsome

This monster who held the ransom
To my gains and my glore
Within two winks of his eye
He silently slithered inside
And with pride he didn't hide
The grin that exposed all his sins!

At that point I pondered
Painfully pointing to my wonder
I stupidly saw in my somber
Where he's been

The enemy's lurking.....

Within.

Nemo me impune lacessit-EAP

I DROPPED MY CROSS AT THE CROSSROAD

I dropped my cross at the crossroad
of His crosses shadow
Where he lighten the burden of my sorrows
And encouraged me to continue through tomorrow
His crosses shadow was my demarcation,
You know, the light touched my face at that location
I shall not turn back to where I came from,
Darkness behind me and the Son before me
through the narrow straight path I stride,
The thorns from my past tear my sides
and the stones of previous mistakes,
Become my journeys stakes
and cause to stumble in my thoughts
And stumble I did as I've fought
thus fall too! I'm telling you
through spring and fall I've traveled through
but what counts isn't the amount
Of scars on my hands and knees,
but the possibility
Of finishing my journey
forward towards eternity
Being the best that I could be

WE HAD CHEMISTRY

So I took your kid home from playtime with mine
and there he is again in your driveway
Version two of your first marriage
you gave me up to be with him
yet you cheated on him with me several times
You're looking for security and the same O same O baby
when you're compromising yourself for chemistry
Well, he's got as much chemistry as baking soda
For you and I baby, I was the gasoline and you the redheaded fire
We had chemistry
the kind that will burn the place down
We had chemistry
the kind people in town will walk around
Talking about for years
We had chemistry
and there was no scientific explanation for it
It was natural and not induce

And now you did it this time again
what you did the first time all over again
you should see it baby
it's déjà vu for you my friend
But not for me
I'm looking for chemistry
the kind that will blow up this town
I'm looking for chemistry
where people will come around
To see me burn

I'm looking for chemistry
the kind that people will be talking about for years
I'm not compromising my chemistry
For false tears

Here you are at the crossroads of your life.
Instead of making a turn or going straight
you went ahead and made a U-turn to your comfort zone.
Husband one version two is what you've got now.
I guess that's what you're looking for
and what you want around.

Adios!

FEAR FROSTED MY FAITH

Fear frosted my faith
falling, fervently I froze in fear
Like Peter pondering walking on water
I started to sink silently in the storm
starving my faith unfaithfully.
Desperately dying to be delivered from despair.
I looked at Him and begged to be saved
not from the stormy salted sea
but from my miserably minded self

Past miracles, marveled and wondered
Erased by the fever-ant fake fear that followed
They held no water to the wait,
that weighted me down

Wondering whether this wait would cease
And my wallowing walk on the water would continue
I asked again,
Haunted, tormented and teary eyed
I painfully prayed to Him and ashamedly asked:
"When will this come to pass?
How long will this last?"
What is this paralyzing pain that protrudes my soul
and this lingering loneliness lusting to destroy me?
When will its end be?
To which, myself sarcastically said onto me:
"At best, when I measure the distance from West to East?"

Above the noise of the crying crowds
shouting screams and wailing words
Shrouded in loud white noise
I heard a whisper!
A fisherman's silken voice
silently saying again…
Relaying:
"let go of the boat.
Let go of your comfort
and walk willingly towards MY right out reached hand".
With my eyes focus and hand reaching out
Right leg paralyzed above the boats wall
I stopped stepping towards
I waited, hesitated...

And what fear kept back.
Faith pushed forward.

OH LORD I NEED YOUR STRENGTH!

Oh Lord I need your strength!
What is the road you've laid before me?
How could this be?
my father just passed at seventy years young
And he hadn't even sung his song
And now I must leave my daughter
to comfort my brother and sisters and others
It was supposed to be our first Christmas
Alone together daddy daughter time at last
Now, will have to pass

My step father is tormented by evil spirits
Please help me stomp them out
and make them quit
He's being scammed by a fortune teller
Who needs to be locked in a cellar
My heart is still coping with my mother's death
Two Christmas' ago.
The pain still lingers,
my heart heals slow
Then my divorce the previous December
Is so close to remember
present problems haunt my mind
Keep freezing me still
all the time
My older kids have abandoned me
And I know not where they be

I need strength!!!
At all length!
Give me strength
To deal with my father's heaven sent
I need strength
To help my step father repent
Give me strength
I'm trying to keep composed,
To close the exposed wounds
of years juxtaposed

Be it more than I can handle
Like an anvil to my ankle
this pain is ample
Please Lord lighten this yoke around my neck.
For I am prostrate
face down on the deck
coping with the weight...

that's making me wait

OH LORD I ASK FOR NOTHING ELSE

Oh Lord I ask for nothing else
but to love and be loved
Loneliness has a toll on me
and his grip is tightening
The silence is substantially shattering
my eardrums
I could no longer loudly hear my heartbeat
I feel pretty paralyzed and alone
my heart is heavy
and my spirit is worn
Again I'm in the midst of the storm

A depression
With north easterly winds
Bringing in a chilling front

Where is she
The one you deemed my soulmate
The one that was supposed to be with me
Forever- my Eve
Why do you delay her
Oh Lord
I must continue this suffering
because...?
I have not the strength of Job
Though I will not condemn thee
Nor forsake thee
Death taunts me

And haunts me
And wants me to give in
Not to forget
About sins forgiven
But to repeatedly replay
Regrettable decisions
and repercussions of romance
The romantic inside
Swore by one million men
That eternity would be
but a wink waiting for the woman I seek
Now is in despair
Desperately deepened decisions
Determine my likeness
To live a lively life
with a worthy wife
Deliver me from my depression
I'm In desperate need to give
My love to live
Well beyond and above
Any common man would dare
To care
And carefully wouldn't commonly give
To any women

.......Anywhere.

Given caution of course.

LORD, WHAT IS THIS CURSE

Lord, what is this curse you laid upon my heart
As weighted down as the stone streets of Stuttgart
The more I try to deliver her from my mind
The more ingrain her touch is intertwined
Every song a memory we shared
Aired to impair my repair
The sun, the moon, the walk in the park
Careless cuddling kisses in the dark

Through my heart
Her whispered words
Wonder like humming birds fly.
"I love you"
"I love you"
"Good bye"
Rang through and through
In a cadence and on queue.
Her love memories float as the leaves falling from the tree
And as plentiful as the blades of grass beneath my feet

My heart is softly saddened
Stupefied in place without a thought
What is this sickness, this cough that I've caught?
Fraught in place
With no speech nor lyrics
I've run out of words I cannot finish
My prayers exhausted
Dehydrated from my tears

Depression is my shadow
It lingers real near
My anorexic dyslexic faith is pushed
And punished to flat line
As my terribly tangled thought try to unwind
My tears are brine onto my wounds
It sets them ablaze as I drown entombed
In this daze...
Of my numbered days....

Gone too soon

ANER HENRIQUEZ

Yes it's another Christmas
3rd one in a row
That happiness evades me
Like a summers snow

First my mother passed
The year before last
A week before her birthday
Who was to know or forecast

Then divorce
Of course
My adult children left with her
And abandoned me
with no reason or why as to be

Now on advent
the morning of Christmas eve
My brother had call me
And together we grieved
Our father had passed
And I listened in disbelief

The small blessing I find
In all this bereave
is my family, sisters, brother,
And cousins you see
For together we sorrow

For our heaven called patriarchs
who touched our lives,
molded us and left their marks.
So my life's lessons learned for all to hear
is hold the ones who touch your hearts....
Close and near.

I love you Pops.
Together we laughed
And made fun of each other.
You poked fun of all of us,
Cousins, sisters and brothers
and you showed me how to relax
and stay calm in the mist of my storms.
To persist forward
To move along
and once again through your persona
Another lesson I see.
Is that you have showed me
at your age of seventy three,
how short life can truly be.

Natividad Henriquez, my mother (who raised me),
Aner Henriquez, my biological dad, her brother.

CHAPTER 5

Illustratum (The light)

When the plane landed in Puerto Rico and I arrived at my stepdad Jose's house, he was pissed that I didn't give him the money for the witch doctor. We barely talked when we saw each other. I slept in my room at night and spent the rest of the day with the family.

But something interesting happened at the funeral. A group of distant cousins that I had never met before (but heard of) were there to pay their respects. They lived in the mountains in at town called Lares. They were sweet, original and authentic believers of Christ. What you saw was what you got with them. We hit it off superfast and super good. And they had invited me to their home in the mountains for New Year's Eve.

First I turned them down, because I felt obligated to be with my brother, sisters, step mom and step dad. Then came the day before New Year's Eve and I had to get away. I had to escape to reset my sanity. I was anxious, and an emotional mess. My brain was about to explode.

Logistically, I was trying to make a one way trip to Lares, then to the San Juan airport. But there were no rental cars available on the island. So I had to take one of my cars and drive it 2 1/2 hours North from Lajas to Lares, and then before I left the island, drive back South (park my car under the house) and then take a 2.5 hour taxi ride from Lajas to San Juan. Logistically and mentally it was a big mess and I really didn't want to spend my last day on the island, on the road that much. But I left to Lares anyway. I had to get away from it all, be in a different surrounding, and spend New Year's Eve of one of the worst days of my life, in the mountains of a tropical paradise.

And man I'm glad I did. When I arrived to Lares, they made me feel welcomed. It was as if I was at home and had never left. Everything seemed familiar, everybody was warm, real, with no reservations, no walls or false pretense. We stood up through New Year's Eve until 2:30 AM, talking and goofing around. That's when I realized that I have actually spent my first New Year's Eve (of the last three years) happy, laughing, swapping stories and enjoying myself, surrounded by my loving Christian family. And it felt great.

The next morning, when I got up, I went to the kitchen for my morning authentic Puerto Rican coffee. I had fresh pastries from the local bakery, and a Puerto Rican egg sandwich (onions, peppers, ham, and mayo on water bread). I asked the girls if they had music, and they went through their salsa list on an iPhone. Then the kids showed up, and I started dancing salsa in the kitchen with the kids. It truly was an incredible time. Words cannot explain the feeling I had being there and associating with them. They have become my new closest family, and I hold them and love them all dearly in my heart. We mourned a lost the day before, but like the prodigal son, they celebrated that they have found me, and I them.

I couldn't tell if my walk in the desert was over. But man, was I glad that I had hit that amazing oasis! And from there on, everything started to get better. Bit by bit. Step by step. Not instantly, but I knew the worst was over. My spirit started to lift up, and I praised God for letting them in my life.

I had hit the bottom, and was riding the bounce back up.

That's when I started writing short stories as well.

SUBMARINE SHORT STORY

Cutting through the waters like a shark's dorsal fin, the blackened salted sail creeps up closer to the crescent mooned sky, leaving a bioluminescent tattle tale trail in its wake.

Beneath the sail, fifty eight breathing souls move as one, as the other seventy eight slumber silently in the submarines belly.

Communicating in code only known by qualified men, the intricate parts of the body move in unison as one, silently slithering onto the surface unnoticed.

As the brain talks to the body, fins, head, and tail, its eyes adjust to the darkness and its ears tune in tightly to hunt for prey.

Sweeping the sky, seeking the unknown in quiet desperation, searching for a fight fathoms beneath the surface, and hunting the horizon, the blackened beast is silently seeking any enemy that might let her release the reality of this raging monster of a machine. All of its sensors are edged on high alert, readily alarming for any contact or orders to wage is wrath upon its enemy.

"Dive make your depth five zero feet"
"Make my depth five zero feet, Dive conn aye!"
"Sonar conn, coming to periscope depth"
"Periscope depth, Con sonar aye"
"Con sonar, baffles cleared"
"So-con aye"

As the beast silently shallows to the surface the tempo of talk accelerates to a quicker beat.

"Con-So new contact designated sierra six"
"So-con aye"
"Raising periscope!"
"Chief raise mast one"
"Raising mast one- aye"

ESM rotate radiate!

Con-esm aye

"So-con, no visible contacts"

"Con esm no contacts"

"Con-so-esm aye"

"Chief of the watch announce on the one MC "surface, surface"

"Chief-con aye....."And he repeats the orders.

"Dive bring 'er up!"

Control, aka Con, is the tactical brain of the submarine, sonar the ears, ESM the radar eyes, Radio its connection to the world.

The "Diving officer" aka Dive, controls the extremities of the boat, and the Chief of the watch (COW) controls the innards, pumping and pushing water and waste with pumps and high pressure air.

Engineering controls the reactor, power, electricity and the propeller to make the sub move, and even though she runs on nuclear power, every now and then they run the giant Fairbanks Morris diesel engine.

Every intricate movement is reported to the CON, the brains of the operation. The con gathers all of the information relayed by the individual stations and moves the boat in accordance with its given orders.

"Chief raise the snorkel mask and announced on the one MC "prepare to snorkel."

Upon the announcement, all parts of the body simultaneously move, expanding, contracting, functioning like the organs and muscles of an Olympian, moving and operating in a harmonious symphony.

She's alive, and on the hunt.

IN THE CIRCLE OF LIFE

In the circle of life
where one end meets the other
to complete ones existence.
Through times persistence
persistently preservers to end our existence.
To delete our past upon our death and disappearance.
The cycle recycles itself as such:
We arise as a thought
Then an encounter is caught
A kiss once naught
Leads to a blessing two sought
A birth
Progressing organic growth
Experiences abundance
A mix of happiness and sadness adds
To our substance
In our reluctance
mortality's loath of immortality
Growing pains lethality
Overtakes our reality
In the end with a new beginning in sight
We become children again.

As we prepare for our heavenly flight.

OH LORD

Oh Lord
To my accord
Take me now!
I implore
Please don't ignore
In a chariot of fire
like you did with Elijah
back in the days of yore

My desire to leave this quagmire
My magnifiers multiplier
is drenched in fears I've acquired
Engulfed in the flames of my past

Now my dried tears spit dust
And my eyes have a crust
Mind nor heart do I trust
That of love's gust
no longer held as just

Hurl me into your presence
present to your persona
Speak to me as with Jonah
Let me smell your aroma
as I enter your Nirvana

Woe my soul to no longer drain
my brain and strength to be stronger

Bear it more, I can, no longer
Please keep me whole once more

As the night gives grief strength
Its a jaguar jumping a fence
To devour my strength at no length
I'm dumbfounded with no sense

So that squandered wisdom be
Won't allow my vision to see
Of freedoms ring from the King
foreseen promised crowns to all that believed
To relieve their grief....

And reward their scared sorrows.

2Kings2

OH WOMEN OF MY PAST

Oh women of my past may ye
lust to be seen with me
So to have my lips taste your dusty bust
As ye feel your girly parts rust
Trussed with thy mind and heart bound
Expounded memories no longer found
Crowned by thy miseries, a mound
an unsound foundation

Like the Thracian's nation now extinct
succinct emotional turmoil
Roil thy royals appearance

Thy wretched seed planted deeply in the soil
Has sprouted a fruitless vine that now coils
and foils thy present love, no longer deep
It holds thy womanhood cheap

Wasted!
Thy fiery passion!
Now lies as a heap of ashen
Unspoken brokenness
hidden beneath thy dress.
Thy minds heart berth.....

An incomplete mess.

AS OF DECEMBER FIRST

As of December first
I came clean
I've put away my vices
and I had decided
to walk to a place
I've seen in my dreams
personated like a picture
covered in lace
Without haste
I'll unveil His purpose to my fate
For as I read Isaiah 6,
affix on His words
"here I am Lord send me"
depicts my purpose
my chord.
Mine which He purchased
through the blood of his Son

As those great men before me
I will humbly travel cliffs hung high
and narrow paths in the valleys
Flooded by tears left behind
blinded by my ignorance
His words will be my deliverance
To concur the curves
that shatter my nerves
and the obtrude obstacles
laid before me.

Through this passion path of victory.

I'd know not where I'd be
for life was a mystery to me.
For once I was Lost,
and now I've found
around the corner of my sins
eternal death wondered through the places I've been

Prostrate before Him
I confessed my sins
and executed my excuses
That laid their lies within

His words were my flicker of lights
in midst of the darkened sky
with no moon lite
Woe to those who know not His words
hide from his sight
and don't crave His touch
As tough as a lion
and gentile as a lamb
He is The Great I AM
For His words keep me calm
and give me Hope to cope

In the midst of my toil
His presence soothed my soul
Like medicine to a bursting boil
He overtook my loneliness like a raging storm

over the sea of Galilee
Me, Submerged in His words
I did conform
Transformed Adrift
in His presence and love.

Before, Like Gideon I was hiding
Abiding my fears thereof
Not knowing the seeds of greatness
He had planted in me
And in the bounty of His harvest
the masses amassed
And in His abundance, He gave
to an unworthy soul as myself
Thy Holy words filled my sails
and relieved my care
In times of depression and despair
The winds whispered His words to my ears
and my mind became clear,
and clearer.

So that when my happiness reflects through my eyes
And the Son's life enters to touch my soul
I can boldly exclaim to the skies:

Blessed is the name of the Lord
Most high!

GOOD SERVICE IS HARD TO FIND

It was Monday morning at 6am, JR had been up all night, with the baby.

Yea, a brand spanking new seven week old girl.

Her little sweaty head gave off an aroma that was addicting to smell, her little fingers felt like gummy worms, and her mouth was always puckered up as if telling the onlooker to "kiss me please".

She was the mini version of her gorgeous mother, with a dimple on her chin.

The smell of Fresh Wipes still lingered in his hands, as he got up for the umpteenth time, after laying her down and placing the pamper in the closable plastic dirty diaper crap can.

His wife had a hard time carrying and delivering the baby, and he manned up and took on one-hundred percent of the chores and responsibilities of the house so that she can rest and recover. He loved her dearly and she meant the world to him. And he'd do whatever it'd take to get her well again.

A migraine had settled in at about 12:30am and he wasn't able to shake it off.

Fists full of Tylenol and anti-histamines hadn't yet battled the war drums beating in his head.

"Crap, its 6:30am. Time to take a shower and get out of here".

He closed the baby's room door, slightly, and walked into his room, to make his way around the bed, not to wake up his wife. As he was walking around the bed he stopped and stared at his beautiful wife soundly slumbering in bed. He bent over and ran his fingers through her thick black hair and kissed her on the forehead and whisper in her ear "I love you sleeping beauty. Daddy will always take care of you". . At that point, in her slumber, he can see the corners of her mouth lift as if she was in a pleasant dream. "Amazing" he thought, at that point he thanked God for how lucky of a man he was. He then reached into the underwear draw (next to his bed), and grabbed a pair of skivvies, that were sitting under his compact Glock 23 handgun, and headed straight into the bathroom, in the dark, closing the door, then turning on the light. The morning ritual was quick as always, along with a few pulling of the nose hairs that fluted out of his Grecian nose, like party favors.

"Shit, that hurts" he murmured under his breath, and headed out of the bathroom and into the kitchen to grab his first cup of coffee. "Ahh, heaven in a cup" he said.

He then opened his laptop to see his first dispatch of the day. "Midtown, Memphis, son-bitch....I'm gonna have to fight that dam traffic."

JR was a DSL installations technician for the tristate area. He roped this job via Monster online. Hired on the spot via a phone interview by the "Silicon Valley DSL" company, getting Silicon Valley pay in Memphis. He was a tech king among his peers, getting paid all of that California money in Memphis, where the cost of living was one third of that of California. This made him a made man to the rest of the Telecom tech's in town.

JR (whose real name was James Richard Jr.) had always been tech savvy. Since he was a kid he'd always take apart the family TV and old radios, to troubleshoot them and see what tubes had burned out inside of them. Then as a young man in the Navy, he became a qualified Sonar tech onboard a US Navy Submarine. That's where he learned micro circuitry and what true patriotism was. In the Navy as a qualified Nuclear weapons watch, he also discovered his love and respect for guns, life and liberty. He was a true conservative. To the right of George Washington, his buddies would say.

"JR, good 'ol George was too liberal for you!" His tech buddy Robbie would always say over an after work craft beer, at the local blue collar watering hole in Cordova.

During his off time (before the baby) he'd help out at the local non-denominational church with the kids, as well with all of the networking of the office computer systems of the church. Setting up the telco router and adding a Cisco switch and firewall to keep the churches network and parishioners safe from viruses and internet trash.

JR truly loved his job, and was ecstatic that he was able to set his work schedule around his wife and new baby. He did it well, and had a great reputation with all of his clients and customers. They'd always call or email the headquarters about how great their experience with the company was and how delightful and informative JR had been. He was the go to guy in his region, and his manager always bragged about him to the higher ups.

But for some reason, today was different. Very odd, and out of the ordinary.

Was it the lack of sleep for the past seven weeks? The screaming politics on the news? Or that his pay increase was cut in half because of the new tax bracket he had just squeezed into… or the accumulation of all of the above and then some.

After diverting a collision at the I-40 and I-240 junction…. Malfunction junction everyone called it, he got onto Sam Cooper Blvd and headed into the historic area of Midtown, where all of the liberals and gays lived. Not that he didn't mind or like them. He was just opposed to them jamming their agenda down the throat of his beloved America. Again that migraine lingered and increased as he got closer to the house he was dispatched to that morning.

In the huge driveway he parked his white Safari van out of the way of the customers Mercedes Benz and Subaru. Just in case any of them had to leave the house. He was always courteous like that.

Upon knocking on the door he was met by a slim beautiful blonde lady. She must have been about thirty-five years old if not younger. She wore Lulu Lemons yoga pants and a sports bra that seemed a bit too small for her endowed bosom.

"Good morning my name is JR, and I'm with the DSL company, are you Mrs. Bee?" JR said with salesman like grin.

"No I'm not. She's my mother, and she'll be right here. I'm glad you came, she's very upset that the service wasn't plug and play as the directions said" she said with a smile, showing her perfectly white straight teeth.

"I just want to warn you, she's a firecracker, and when she's not happy, the whole world is not happy". Carole, as she was called, had stopped by her widowed mother's house to check on her. She was extremely sweet, pleasant and courteous, and even offered JR a bottle of water. Which he turned down politely.

She pointed JR in the general direction of where the DSL box was located, then called her mother down again, and left the house to her Pilate's appointment.

The old house and its furnishing and décor were stuck in time. It was truly a museum piece of the 1960's, opulently decorated for it era, smelling like moth balls and old dust.

The introduction to Mrs. Bee was short and quick, and she lead JR to her office on the first floor, where she had stacks of papers and books piled on the floor, her desk, and every bit of shelf space in the twelve by ten foot sized room. She was a proper southern women, in jeans, Birkenstocks and a button up sweater. Under the sweater you can see her red Che Guevara t-shirt that her granddaughter had gotten for her last Christmas, and you can see the blonde had washed out of her shortly cropped grey hair. You can tell that she was a very well kept lady who was possibly in her mid to late 70's. She spoke proper English, with a Memphian accent.

On the walls she had framed signed pictures of various democratic political hopefuls, politicians, and influence shufflers. Some current and others faded and aged a bit with time and sunlight. Mrs. Bee was a retired Civil Rights lawyer, and continued to be a main mouthpiece with the local political hacks in the mid-south.

As JR got closer to the room, it was as if someone had put a cloth pin on his nose. The breathing through his nose completely shut down and he stated to breathe through his mouth.

"Excuse me Mrs. Bee, do you have any long haired cats?" he was extremely allergic to them and could barely breathe when they were around.

"Why yes I do, but he's in the other room"

"Ma'am, I'm allergic to cats, but I'll do the best I can while I still can. If that is OK?"

"What do you mean? You better fix the problem! I've paid good money for this service."

"Yes ma'am I will do my best" JR said as his eyes started to itch.

As he followed the telephone line around the room, behind a bookcase, then under her desk, he could see that the jack was dated back to when they had the rotary phones, so he replaced it, hoping that the jack was the reason the light on the DSL router didn't blink green. But it wasn't. He'd now have to search all over the house and attic for all of the jacks and figure out the layout of the wiring scheme of the telephone lines. "Shit" he thought, "I really don't want to be here. I'll have to call one of the other guys to finish this job, or I'll need an Epipen to get out alive".

By this time, the migraine had gotten to the point where all he could hear were the veins on the side of head pulsating. The cat hair didn't help at all. His breathing became shallow, his eyes red and teared. He felt as if he had a fur ball clogging his throat.

This was it, he wanted to throw up! He had had it and he had to leave NOW! The migraine and his allergic reaction to the cat hair had him in a complete fog of pulsating pain. As he was trying to get up he stared up at her, stammered and lost his step as the vertigo set in. He fell back down on his knees. In a short breath he told her he had to leave.

Her face turned red, and she raised her left hand shaking her pointing finger at him and got in his face as he was still trying to get up. JR couldn't make out what she was saying, it sounded like the teachers voice in a Peanuts cartoon. "waap, waa waa…"

Her voice linger in his mind like a long winded foghorn, off of a San Francisco shore. She now, commenced to screaming at him. While his thoughts were trying to unscramble her words, he stared at her mouth. His head throbbing, hands shaking, and the spit foam from the corner of her mouth, squirted onto his face. "Good service is hard to find these days! YOU ARE NOT LEAVING HERE UNTIL YOU FIX IT- DAMMIT!!!"

It was a reflex reaction. Like swatting a mosquito on his arm.

The Glock 23 drew from his belt holster, in the small of his back. He always carried it after almost being car jacked on Parkway and Elvis Presley Blvd. He then quickly pointed it to her head, and slowly squeeze the trigger for what seemed like an eternity.
BOOM!
It was done.

Now his mind and nose cleared up, the headache went away and he was able to breathe again. He stood up from the kneeling position he had taken under her computer desk.
"-bout time you shut the f**k up! Now I can think" he told the limp body, with the protruding hole on the side of her head.
"Dammed liberal b***h. You're probably a Hillary supporter and an Oprah and Whoopi watcher.
Ya gun snatching, tax raising, entitlement wanting, s**t!
Feed the world with other people's money, but what about the problems here in –Merica. "
"F**king liberals are going to tax the hell out of the middle class, and are gonna pass a bill banning our God dam guns. What the hell is this country coming to?"

He holstered his weapon, then picked up his tool bag and walked out of the house, closing and locking the front door.
He placed a door tag on the door handle, "SVC DSL: Missed appointment, reschedule required. Please contact our help desk at 1-888-555-1212 for a new appointment".
"There ya go. I hope they bill you twice. Good service is hard to find? Huh.
I bet, with an attitude like that," he mumbled to himself.

As he walked down the walkway of the front of the house, the sun shone bright and the mocking birds were out in full shout. It was music to JR's ears. He loved hearing birds sing, especially the Cardinals and Robins that were scratching the ground and plucking the morning worms from the manicured front lawn of this lovely historic house. He really admired this 1890's structure, especially the stained glass entry.

He hit the auto door locks to open his van, and left the driveway towards his second dispatch.

"I hope the next customer isn't as nasty and rude as she was." He thought to himself.

WHY I DON'T WRITE BEAUTIFUL THINGS ANYMORE

My heart is too scared to love
My emotions too tattered to feel
My vision too clouded to see

There is no heaven above
Nothing's real
Not the birds nor the bees

Shoved off into darkness
Reel in hand
Sea awaits my retrieval

Of all this starkness
Teal salted sands
Conceived my upheaval

Hook caught in my glove
Knotted line in my reel
There'll be no fishing of hearts for me

It all seems surreal.

SPRING IS HERE

Spring is here
and sprung it did
the flowers are placing their bids
the grass is turning in little bits
from brown to green
A change In the landscape scene
For which I can't ignore

But be foretold.
for me winter still lingers
Like a chill between my toes
chilling memories unfold
My heart is a mass of ice
No device or advise
can defrost this darkened stone
anymore

As the suns strikes, it still remains cold
Afar in the park children play like prancing foals
In delight and laughter on this gray
spring day with a full moon in fey
Their happiness unfolds

Alone on the brown grass I inverted
The disasters I've averted
In relationships skirted,
With all the hearts I diverted, concerted
Then deserted for reasons I know no more.
I knew no more, as I sat there on the cold grassy floor.

In my shadow a raven landed
and he stood there very candid
and he, to me, did scorn
the feelings I had mourned
nor was I fore warned
of the things he had to say.
And he said them to my dismay.
"Happily unhappy" he implored
He implored then said no more

"What?
What say you, you tarred fowl?"
I scowled and looked around,
Feeling like a clown,
a sad clown sitting on the ground,
on the parks floor.
Happily unhappy" he retorts
as I got up from the floor
on my feet and stared him down
where he laid
"How can ye proclaim this fate?"
...my yarrow, torments, displeasures of my discernment's gait
The thoughts of unraveled relationships that pest me like thrips
through the nights
Bypassing my windows screens and doors

"Happily unhappy" he repeats
As his words sink in and seep,
Seep into my core...
Like nothing that's happened before.

"Fly away you darkened monster!

Shoo, back to the corn fields you've conquered!
Have your words with a scarecrow
and let him ingest your fowl woes
Leave me be! Leave me alone once more!"
I scuffed and re-sat on the grassy floor

Then, with his beady eye he stared my face
a yard or two taking his place.
He said nothing piercing my disgrace
without a word I knew not what he was thinking for whom and
what for...
What for? Whilst sitting on the floor

In my thoughts I kept sinking
Am I delighting in my demise?
Who is this profitless profit that stopped by?
A freak of nature conspiring against me?
Claiming my feelings by decree?
By decree as if by law.

As I Sat there sinking in my aught
Almost in slumber,
I forethought the words he brought,
and what I encumbered....
Was my own deception the exception
of my perception?
Or is it just a lore?
Just a lore and nothing more?

With a twist of his head
As if nothing was said
He leaped into his flight

And took off into the sky
Without a care of the moments of yore
Moments of yore I thought, as I sat on the brown grassy floor

"Come back!" I scowled
"Comeback again!"
And tell me, what you meant
Was it God or devil ye were sent!
To repent of my discontent.
Were you sent to torment?
Sent to torment me, once more?

He festered this heart that's spent,
with words that bore its content.
Am I to repent of my discontent
and my creation of indignation?
In this springs hours hoar.

In the distance a billboard reads,
That which my eyes can't believe
The thing I see, can't be unseen.
The answer to which I seek a cure
an ad that reads.... "Sure".
It reads sure, to my deplore.
My answer on the billboard,
warmed my heart and nothing more.

CYBER LOVE

When it comes to love
I'm a habitual offender
Don't try to stop me
because I'll never surrender
You love me
you hate me
you want me
you crave me
Poets loathe me
Because my feelings are so tender
Kids hear it
And write it
Then bite it
and rap it
because my words are lyrical
When I touch your hand girl It's all so magical
I kiss your lips girl and you become hysterical
You love me
you hate me
you want me
you crave me
I look in your eyes
and you want to violate me

The night is still young hon
it's only 8:30
We're dancing at the club
And you're being real flirty
You touch me
You kiss me

You squeeze me
To please me
And press your body onto mines, because you're getting real
Horney

Now we're in my car
And we're going to your place
You're acting real wild, with that crazy look on your face
I'm driving
You're dancing
Then diving
We're chancing
I'm hoping I won't wreck my car and we get there alive

I'm tensing
I'm swerving
Dispensing
Observing
the road ahead, while you release your crazy sex drive
Your fantasies come true girl, and you want to keep me with you.
I'm a free spirit child
and I have to move to my groove
you disapprove girl because I'm driving away from your place.
You text me
You call me
Facetime me
And skype me
Feeling lonely,
you're crying,
despising the moment you fell in love though cyberspace.

DEAR BELOVED

Dear beloved
Though this day
I cannot be swayed
That this is such an unjust world we live in
where the balance of life is misaligned and unforgiving
playing like an untoned Violin
Those who love with their hearts
are entrenched with those that don't know how to love and
appreciate the other
as a whole with in.

They know not what it's like
to love ones quintessence
Only the flesh and desires untrue
if you were just a particular essence
I would've easily forgotten you
Placed our memories on a shelf
and replaced you with someone else
But here in my heart you are
like a fence post grown over by a tree
You have become and irremovable piece of me
that which will always be embedded inside
Which To remove would mean that I'd die

My love is as visible as Venus in the moonless sky
Afar, a shimmering light
It reflects your radiance
shown upon my souls delight

Be I bold enough to say
that if I had to wait
10 thousand years for our hearts to meet again
I would boldly fain
10 thousand fold
And endure the pain

I WISH I WAS KISSING YOU

I wish I was kissing you
instead of missing you.
Watching the red curls in your hair
Instead of staring into the air
Seeing your nose crinkle when I say a funny
The passion in your voice, when you called me "honey"
The way you smile when you lie in my bed
Deeply focused on the words I've said
I know you're self-conscious about your curves
But to me you're more than a masterpiece,
And I wonder if I'm worthy of what I observe.

when I wake and see you asleep by my side
It's amazement and luckiness I feel inside
And my heart beats intensely when you enter the room
There is no greater beauty that looms
When you giggle, smirk, and let out a glee
We both bust out, on a laughing spree
When we cuddle and your head is on my shoulder
Makes me feel so much braver and bolder
Your milky white skin, against my tanned flesh
Makes a perfect contrast, I confess
When I pick you up to take you out on a date
My breath gasps, cause you increase my heart rate

Am I cruel and selfish for not to wanting to leave your side?
For I want to love and savior the moments,
…..before we say "good bye".

IT WAS AN UNEXPECTED THING

It was an unexpected thing
this that happened to me
Who would've guessed it to be?
Or who would've fore seen?

Green lace contrasted her milky skin
Her angelic face lead me in
her sweet voice was calming
She had blue eyes and hair of almond
She wiggled when she walked
And called me d-hhharling
when we talked

As I entered her room, content
I took a whiff of a familiar scent
Scents of Prada and Blue, filled the air
it held me there, as if in a snare

Electric Green Stiletto heels
She smiled and revealed
her perfect teeth
And some girly parts beneath
With that conservative librarian look
She was formative
and wrote my name in her book.

I'm jonesing over her love and touch
As if a lot, is never enough

CHAPTER TEN

In pain, no medicine to take
my soul crumbles and aches
deep in the capillaries of my heart
The life that flowed within
Was taken apart

Who would've known
that she'd set me up for such a hard fall
And left me broken up
No pieces repairable.
Nothing at all

She's a serial killer
a television chiller
Aiming straight for the heart
And I became a filler....

Just another mark on her chart.

MY DEAREST

My dearest;

When we first met
I knew not how important
you'd become to me
Just a girl I thought
Make love to her
then she'll be on her way
Till this day, I'd say
you blew me away

For the moment we were together
We were two imperfect people
Learning true love from each other
refusing to give up on one another
Overcoming obstacles
And dreaming the possible.

What happened my dear?
Was the timing wrong
did you become weary
was my love too good to be true
did you think the fantasy was false?
You had said I was everything you wanted in a man
"A specimen with a heart so perfect..."
I don't understand?

CHAPTER FIVE

SHORT STORY- VANS APPLE PIE

It's been a long time a coming.

The Lowe clan had embarrassed the Valanbooth family long enough.

Van Valenbooth the 5th had been living in his log home he had built himself for over thirty years now.

The trees used for his home were the same ones that his ancestors planted centuries ago.

He had found one in the middle of the woods, down by the dried up creek with the initials of VV&HL surrounded by a heart.

They were the same initials of his great, great grandpa and grandma, and he figured that he's make that the main beam of the vaulted ceilings. So when folk came to visit he'd had a great historic story to tell, when he pointed up to the heart on the beam and would begin to wax his tale. And a story teller he was. When politicians would hold town hall meetings to get folks vote, they'd call on him to lead the introduction of the new political speaker.

Sometimes the pastor would ask him to lead the church in prayer.

And when he did it was as if the Lord was speaking in your face through him, mind body and soul.

As for the political gigs, he had no side. He always said the best side was the one that paid the most. And those political gigs landed him a lot of money.

He wouldn't say what, but every eight years he'd get him a new Ford f-250 truck Texas edition. And he'd drive to Texas to get it. Those political ties also helped keep the local Sheriff out of his business.

Every time a raid was setting up, he'd get a call, with enough time to shut down and move his moonshine operation.

People around here said that Van Valenbooth was an accomplished man in everything he'd done. Except for one.

His oldest daughter (Christie) was a doctor in Boston. She had won Miss Appalachia at the county fair three times in a row, which lead her to get a scholarship at Boston University. Valanbooth's and the entire community were so proud of her, that every time someone would ask about Christie, Vans face would glow with pride. The middle boy, Joseph was a Naval officer, and the youngest, Thomas, was an executive for a wireless company. The entire Valenbooth kids did a whole lot better than their kin and the Lowe family. But the kids left a long time ago. And would only visit at least two or three times a year with the children in tow to eat some of moms great homemade cooking.

Whether it was Thanksgiving, Christmas, or Van and Sarah Kate's birthday, they'd make it home. Except for now. When his beloved Sarah Kate had passed away a few years back, and the kids kind of stopped coming and started calling more. They'd ask Van to move in with them, but Van wouldn't have it.

Who was going to take care of the land and upkeep Sarah Kate's grave? No one could have done that any better than Van.

Besides, the neighbors had always asked him for some of Grandma Valenbooth's apple pie moonshine. Who was going to run the family business? Van had a knack for making the stile and cooking the goods, as it was done one hundred years ago, over a hickory fire. Depending on the time of year and the brew he was making he could get as much as $50 to $100 a bottle. Especially after the tasting contest at the county fair. Until Charley Lowe stole his grandma's apple pie recipe. It had been in the family for over one hundred years. Grandma had hand stitched it onto one of her cooking smocks and kept it hid in a hope chest she was given as a girl.

Van didn't know how Charlie had gotten the mix for her brew, but his shine tasted almost exactly like Vans and sometimes better depending on the season and the pickings of the ingredients and wood.

During the last five county fairs, the Lowes apple pie came in first and Van's second. And this time Van had had enough. Since Sarah Kate had been gone, Van stewed revenge for ol' Charlie Lowe. Something in his blood seemed to call it out. It was as if it was naturally bred in him. He had to punish with impunity. The ghost of his kin's past demanded it. And he had to do it in a way that no one would ever suspect it was his good friend Van.

The Lowe family was fierce, and were a force to recon with. They were also highly respected, with young Timmy Lowe as the mayor and his wife Jenny as the county clerk. They had the local Sherriff (who was their cousin) in their pocket, and Charlie brought the pride back in the family with his new stolen Apple pie shine.

Now Van had a lot of time to think. All of that time alone with quietness and solitude can get to a man. And he was no exception. He'd run his plot on the opening day of the county fair, August 22nd, right after the judges met to taste and classify each families brew. Fair week was like Black Friday for folks in the shine business. That's when people would come in from all over the state to buy some from the locals and that meant that the winner of the fair could ask any price he wanted for his shine. Usually whatever the market would bare, and most of the city folks would pay up to two hundred dollars per bottle, depending on how money dumb they were.

Charlie used to be a judge, until five years ago when he started to enter Lowes family Apple Pie shine. And still to this day, with his pride on his sleeve and a lifted brow, he goes around tasting everyone's brew, classifying it to his liking, and rating it.

And by about ten at night, Charlie was usually pretty lit up. To the point that he could hardly walk or talk.

That's when Van will approach him and take on the family's revenge. Once and for all ridding another low down Lowe from this county.

As always, Charlie was walking through the fair with a Ball jar in his hand. He had just walked out of a tasting tent staggering and singing "A Boy Named Sue", with slur speech. It was about 9:46 pm, right on time.

Charlie, ol' friend, how ya dew-in?

Van! Van you old goat how ya doing?

Great buddy, but you wouldn't believe what I just cooked?

Don't tell me another stash of that Valenbooth rut gut? Hahahah."

He laughed out loud, so hard the third button on his plaid flannel shirt popped out.

Well ol friend, I changed the receipt. And I think that next year it will take the prize. But one thing.

I need your advice and taste buds to see if I got it right. I added a twist to it, and was wondering if it would be to the judges liking.

Well, where is it? Let me get some and I'll tell you right now.

Well, Charlie, I didn't want to mix it up with what I was selling out of the truck, so I left it where I brewed it, to let it chill and work itself up for a bit.

Where….Where? Bring it to me now and I'll taste it. I'll tell you if its worthy of your Families name.

Buddy I can't ask you to do that now. Enjoy yourself with the other Lowes and have fun at the Carnival. I heard that Nana's fried turkey legs are reeeal guuud!

No! Bring it to me now.

Charles Lowe, it's in a secret place in that mine shaft we used to play in when we were kids at the base of Sugar Head Knob. It's too dark and far to go there now. And I'd hate to see you get hurt walking through the woods in the dark.

Besides you're drunk and don't look too well. And you probably won't be able to make it there in this darkness. I'll ask one of the judges to give me their opinion. Maybe Carl McCants can tell me.

Nonsense! I've walked those woods with my eyes closed a hundred times. Carl couldn't tell the difference between dish water and beer. I don't know why the hell they let him judge. Come on! Let's go!

Seriously Charlie?

Dammit yea! Come on.

As Van lead him through the woods with the mini flashlight he carried on his keyring, his soul stirred and he felt a chill down his back as all the hairs stood on the back of his neck. Charlie kept on singing and mumbling the words to the song as he sipped the Ball jar.

"Charlie be careful, we're almost at the mine". Van said with concern in his voice.

"I know…Where is it?" Charlie demanded.

"It's about 50 feet inside the mine, behind a rock pile, you don't think I'd want someone to stumble upon it? Do ya"? Van said sarcastically.

"Well lead the way"

Ya know Charlie, maybe this is a bad idea. They closed this mine up because of all of the men that died in here. I'll just bring you some in the tomorrow, or just let Carl taste it later.

"NO! Get out of the way. Beside Carl doesn't know s**t! A toast to the dead and the ones that gave their lives to make a living!" Charlie said as he spilled the last of the shine in the Ball jar on the sacred ground as a remembrance to the dead in that mine. He tossed the jar onto the rock walls shattering it, and then continued into the mine leading the way now through the darkness.

About sixty feet into the mine, behind a knee wall of rocks there lied three stacks of wooden crates. All full of Ball jars.

"Bingo!" Charlie shouted. And he continued singing louder.

Charlie opened a crate, and pulled out a Ball jar and screwed off the lid.
Cheers! A toast to the souls resting in this mine.
Van picked up another jar, opened it and followed with his own toast.
Cheers Charlie, may you live long enough.
And they both took swigs of their own jars.

Drink up Charlie, and taste the other crate. I made this batch with a twist in the receipt. Let's see if you can tell the difference.

As Charlie bent over, he stumbled onto the crates, all of the alcohol had started to wear him down. So he shut his eyes for about a second or so.
At that time Van placed a short chain around his ankle, and pad locked it tight. Earlier that week Van had hammered a piton into a low boulder in the wall and secured a three foot chain to the piton with another pad lock.

Charlie then bellowed out when he opened his eyes, as if regaining consciousness.

Hahaha! Is this a joke? Just like when we were kids, aye Van? You got me ya d**khead.

Now what the hell are you going to do with me?

And Charlie continued to sing with his eyes closed, slurring every word, and skipping a few.

As Charlie was singing, Vann turned around and started walking out of the mine.

As Vann walked out, he pull the rope that was holding an old rotted beam up, that kept the ceiling from caving in.

With every step he took you can hear Charlie' slurred singing and the overhead crumble.

By the time he walked out of the cave there was a huge rumble. Dirt and dust shot out of the entrance, covering Vann's entire back and hair. Then there was a giant quite. As if noise was sucked up by a big black hole. No singing, no crickets, or night birds. Just a tremendous deafening quite, as if the entire world had just caved in.

As Vann was walking down the hillside back to the fair, in his head, he can still hear ole Charlie singing that stupid country song.

"F**k you Charlie! He said out loud to himself.

F**k you".

I'M A WRECK

I'm a wreck and a skeptic
about to become unglued
because I knew
your love was untrue
We broke up on Tuesday at around four o'clock
And On Friday
you placed him in my spot
on your bed
Regardless of what you said
Your co-dependency screams ahead
"I need some time to be alone in my home.
Single with no one to mingle"
What a bunch of BS
As if I wouldn't have guess this mess
If only you would have been honest and committed
To the words you said
Instead of clinging onto the illusions of safety in your head

You see
for I am me
And can never be
Nor will ever be
someone else.
For I am a sure man
With dignity
And responsibility
To myself
Adios!
I'm done with you!

YOUR LIGHT ILLUMINATES THE SKY

Your light illuminates the sky
And when the desert is dry
Your love reigns over the rain
And like a celebration with champagne
The flower rejoice by choice
For they too have free will to praise
And beautifully bloom throughout the day
In the morning the birds awake in their worship songs
And pass their plainsong lyrics to their young, lifelong
In flight they dance their praise
Sparrows, swallows, sandpiper with its shades of grey

Your heart consumes my woes
Because of it, I fear no foes

If I had three tails I'd wag them all
Winter, Summer, spring and fall
For you are the joy to this little boy
Comforting as a baby blanket and favorite toy
If I would ever to lose this voice
I'd have no choice
But beat the rocks until they rejoice,
and please us
When they call your name:
Jesus, Jesus, Jesus

Because of you my story is greater then I
For had I not you, it would've died

But I live beyond my chances
my circumstances didn't matter
And my sins you did shatter
So pain turned into joy
And rebuilt this life once destroyed

My life's renewed Because of you
I'm no longer askew, Because of you
I've made it through, Because of you

....Jesus, I love you.

MY QUEEN IS NOT THE FAIREST OF THE LAND

My Queen is not the fairest of the land
For her hands have tiled fertile land
Her feet are as big as a cyclops head
And they sometime drag as if full of lead
When she walks her gait goes flop flop flop
And when she runs, she has a funny hop hop hop
Her curly hair always matted in a bun
And the buttons to her blouse are always missing or undone
She has more wrinkles on her clothes then to her hands and face
Oh let me tell you about our place!
She doesn't know how to keep the house clean
it's dusty with webs through every space it seems
When she laughs she snorts
All sorts of stuff comes out of her snout
and her big bosoms shiver and quiver
When She laughs out loud
And raw liver she eats for her daily snack
And with her breath she'll give you a smack
And as age has done her a tremendous injustice
When she can't find things she fusses up a ruckus
Sometimes she forgets to put the children's lunches in their
backpacks
So they raid other kids lunch boxes and lunch sacks

Be she raunchy and flawed as your eyes have seen.
She'll always be...

.....my beautiful Queen

I NEED TO DIE

I need to die
To regain my life
For life without death
Will belie the decry of living
So am I truly living?
For my death, my burdens were lifted
His gift to me went unspoken
As the gift shifted from His grace
To my soul
My self-manifested destiny
Is now over.
As my hands grow older
My dreams did die younger.
I'm walking in my weakness
Through all this bleakness,
My meekness over powers me.

Living off of the scraps from the ravens
In this tragic haven
The only thing I have is poverty
And that too resides in paucity
And I have given that quandary

My giants have off springs
And without a doubt
They have come to seek me out
Not a moment was acquired
Now that my youth expired.

For my giants have rallied
The Amorites seek me in the valley
The Jesuits occupied my home
The Hittites continue to roam
Putting out a hit on me

Even though persecution surrounds me
And there is nowhere to flee
I am cornered but not concurred.
Hidden like Elijah
Embolden like Jeremiah
Here I hide, among my captors
At the end of my old chapters.
My tears and worries
Were placed on the cross
And with His mercies
A new page lies before me
Like a squall
His grace ….

Will write it all.

I LOVE MY WHITE JACKET

I love my white jacket
it's fashionable where I live
everyone wants one
Especially the cool kids

buckles on the back
straps on the arm
It keeps me safe
from hatred and harm

There are many like it
But this one is mines
They make me wear it
All of the time

My roommate compliments me
He says it clashes well with my skin
The nurses tighten the straps
Every time they come in

CHAPTER 6

Sanitatum (Healing)

During this chapter (6) was when the healing started to manifest itself in my life.

After attending Hope church for a while, taking notes in all of the sermons, and associating with people of like mindedness, I began to understand that my relationships with other people was placed before my relationship with God. In a way, I was practicing idolatry. Putting my relationships with women (my idols) before God.

It began with an image in my mind that became an illusion, a false perception in my head that became my idol (the thing I focused on, and needed badly). Every time I tried to make someone become something else they weren't meant to be, I was performing idolatry. I could read it in my poems, in my actions with the women, and in my false perception of the ladies I had dated. Even though they were great in certain aspects, I wasn't able to see their flaws and they weren't able to acknowledge mine, until it was too late, and the relationships came crashing down and blew up. I notice that I was actually creating my own emotional bride of Frankenstein. I was taking the pieces of this person, and that person, and added the personality of another to create the soul mate of my dreams in my imagination, and none of them fit, because that person didn't exist. Because God makes people in HIS image not mines! I had stayed in my bad marriage because I felt that I had invested too much in that relationship to quit. I had the yoke of complacency around my neck and it kept me from being who God made me to become. Sometimes you have to let some people go to reach your destination. You cannot carry their weight/wait to your destiny. Bad relationships must come to an end in order to move forward to the next chapter in your life. I had to admit to myself and God, that what I was trying wasn't working, and I had to humble myself and do His will, even though it didn't make sense to me. One thing I also learned was my transition from an old chapter in my life to the new one was full of warfare. Sometimes that's where we get stuck, in the struggle. It becomes too emotionally and physically hard and draining. So we quit!

During the season of change there is no instant gratification. You have to leave the last chapter's luggage behind, and come into your new season with a new level of hunger and a new diet. You cannot sustain your new season living off of the old diets from your previous season. An example of this is when we grow up and graduate from high school. You no longer can live on cereal and Twinkies. You have to eat adult food, or you will suffer the consequences in your health.

I came back to Memphis from Puerto Rico with my life repurposed. I no longer lived with Anxiety (trying to control my future) and depression (trying to control my past). I started to understand why I had gone through what I did. Why my relationships failed. Why my finances failed. Why I was distant from God, and why I had gone through this desert. It was to depend on Him and get closer to him. When you understand your why, it redefines your life and purpose. In all, it was a spiritual, mental and emotional build up to begin to receive his blessings.

And now, I understood that the lessons, were the blessings. And the blessings poured in after I was prepared for them.

And so, with my spiritual walk renewed, I continued. And here are the thoughts and poems that manifested themselves during this journey.

MY PAST FAILURES

My past failures follow me
flawlessly around
Through the creased corners
of my eye
I see them silently and slowly
shadow me throughout the town
I prayed to the Lord to help me
rid them now
His reply bewildered me
and raised my brow

"Son. I avow,
as the Sun seeps through the sky,
I placed them there
so you won't forget why
you're rid of your sins.
So don't invite them back in
For if you do, and you stray
they will gather in masses
like a Giants parade

"But Lord I am in agony
and I am deeply afraid"
he replied,
"what makes you any different
than Esau, Job or Jacob?
With his coat that looks like a robe?
Think ye not they felt the same

with their suffering and pain?"

Be patient my son
for this victory is won
and your season of suffering
will soon be done.

And because those words
stay ingrained in my brain...

I no longer complain.

OH SWEET MOTHER

Oh sweet mother, my dear
it's been several years
Since you've gone away
on a Tuesday like today

Oh how I miss your laughter
till this day and after
Seeing your smile
hearing your humor beguile

The smell of your skin
And the way you used to call me in
as I played in the streets,
At the door your hug would greet.

As a young boy
you used to dress me in suits
and white knee socks-oh joy
and Buster Brown boots

I was always in style
Unlike any other child
and British school cap is what I wore
and yes, I still have my Mets uniform

Adore you and it I will,
Until the day my body chills
Then with you I'd be
Embraced in God's loving will.

MY HEART

My heart's in asylum
Sheltered from the rain
Behind these walls
it's trying to sustain

No communication
from the outside world
No one can reach it
not even the girls

Medicating itself
from the fallout pain
Expectations never met
Would drive any man insane

The elephants are looking in
From the peep hole outside
This room will keep me safe
Its padded in white on every side

TO MY OWN BENEFIT

To my own benefit
my paradigms and prejudices
have gone awash

the words I once stood on
are bygone.
They became my quicksand

And I could not withstand
the unplanned consequences
of their offenses

motionlessly sinking
inch by inch
they cause me to think

And rethink the beliefs
that I once clinched
With no relief

In a cinch
I released them from my fist
And dismissed them I did

to no longer subsist
The narrow thoughts
that weighed me down

And almost caused me to drown
In this emotional quicksand
that was all around

PEOPLE ARE LIKE FLOWERS

People are like Flowers and stones
There are those that are radiant with fragrance
bringing beauty and smiles to the world
Then others that are measured by the days temperature
Sunny hot,
cloudy cold,
rainy wet

But Gods love is like the bee that pollinates the flower
Forever vigilant
He encourages us to grow,
And his grace is as the morning rain
It washes our sins away drop by drop
Weather be it flower or stone
We are all cleansed by his grace

SUBMARINERS PRIDE

Tomorrow is Memorial Day again
and my hat goes off to the Iron men
who served before me, with me, and after me.
For now I reflect upon the sea's decree.

To the submariner's whom I rode with
and went through some "awe s**t" moments (Patrol 69)
and got through them- alive.
No better crew could ever hold their heads up so high

For on that day, Neptune marked us to die.
As water entered the people tank we wagered and savored the
danger.
To death, we dared to stare in its wicked eye
to laugh and crack jokes as we dried.

Undenounced to Neptune's pleasure
We dared to keep the Scorpion and Thresher
In port and starboard watches
In the deep oceans pressure.

No greater crew could God had mustered then or after.
Than the men who survived that disaster.
The submariner's creed, "Steel boats, Iron men",
could have never manifested itself ever so better than then.

For this ye shall always be my brothers.
Salted men of the deep!

For in silence Das Boats will always creep
As we seek one another.

Gods speed with you all!
It was an amazing ride.
And as Neptune moves the tides
we'll always answer our call

....with Pride.

LO-DEBAR

Oh lord
my disabilities are vagrant
my courage is non-existent
Lo-debar stays steadfast in my mind
How do I remove it?

Please tell me,
please be kind.
You've healed me from my wounds
And I seek your direction
Because I'm blind

And in faith
I've moved
forward to presume
That my past sins won't catch up with me
As the night with the moon

Like a storm coming via the sea
the separation anxiety
I fear from letting go
Has left me out of fuel
And now, I feel low....

...and miniscule.

2Sam9:4-5

GOD IS NOT DONE WITH ME YET

Scares and wounds exposed
Hauntingly hungry for a word of worthiness
Staring into the obis of darkness
Waiting for death to overtake me
Barely living off of scraps of hope

In the cold unforgiving street of despair
Where no soul cares
Sitting on the edge of disaster
Dazed, willing to collapse
A relapse my souls willing to allow

No good feelings now
can tame the loneliness that comes after
These words came to set
The beginning of my end of regret
with my mind hereafter

"God is not done with me yet"
As they whispered in my minds ear
Why would He take mercy
on a dead dog like me?
This is not clear.

Why is it that hurt people hurt me?
For this I cannot see
Nor any fallible reason believe
Know they not the destruction they've conceived?

Crippled like Mephibosheth
Awaiting a sudden death
Royalty in my blood
Paid for me from above
A table never known to me, existed

And its worthiness, I resisted
My self-talk was my frenemy
Taking the best of me
leading me to abandon any hope
I'd given to myself

As destiny rotted on my shelf
Till this day
as I crept forward and away
in my pain
These words I hear

Real clear, so not to veer
From my hearts claim
That "Gods not done with me yet"
And with His promise
I forget my regret.

WHO AM I?

I'm the guy that runs into a burning building
while everyone else is running out.
I'm the guy that runs towards gunfire
while the rest are running away.
When I hear a baby cry
I can soothe it with a lullaby.
When our planes fly in missing man formation.
I tear up
For the people sacrificed for this nation.

I'm the veteran who salutes our flag
When she parades on by.
My knees get week
and tears stream down my cheeks
when I hear the national anthem
Because I know the sacrifice
that was made to keep our country free
I protect old glory
Because she holds many stories
Of men like me who wore her as a symbol of hope
on their arm patches in foreign lands and afloat

When other nations gave lip service
that they cared.
I showed up and was there
To feed the hungry
Cloth the naked
Shelter the homeless

Relief to the wounded
And lift up the weary

I'm the God fearing soul
that volunteers at church
I'm the cub master
who teaches little boys honor
The father that sacrificed a child
On foreign land in war
The employee who gets up at 4:30am
To be early at work or pray for a friend

The store clerk with the helpful smile
The doctor who works long hours
The farmer who prays for rain showers
I am a dream that became reality
To a rag tag group of armed
Businessmen and farmers
I am America
The land of the brave
And home to the free

Who the hell are you?

WAR

The stench of fear is in the air.
All hearts changed.
No longer do they feel.
No one cares.
Each side swears
the other is evil.
Damn the adults who started
this upheaval!

Oaths taken
cannot be broken by pens.
Causes and reasons
distributed by peaceful men.
Bullet casings
become puddles of blood.
Who can tell
when enough is enough?

Riffles blast into the air.
Peaceful souls descend and hide
as evil looms
through the night.
The revolution is coming!
No, it's here!
Come and see!
The gunshots sound near!

In the doorways

children tremble in fear.
Will there ever be an end
to this bloodshed?
Will there ever
be peace instead?
Their youth and innocence
sacrificed, stained and stolen.

Bolden by money,
eyes full of green,
peddle fear.
Politicians and profiteers
wallow in their wealth
as they load their accounts in stealth.
Know they not the trouble they've cause?!?

Haven't they heard the tears before?!?

Praying for deliverance
now that evil's around
a child can no longer
stand his ground.
So he asks God
to extract his woes,
to come guard
and save his soul.

As feeling unravel
gunshots crackle.
The wounded babble

at the sight of spent shells.
War is hell.
Evil, is its smell.
It's no place for children

.....to live or dwell.

I WOKE UP AT THREE

I woke up at 3:30 this morning
I was mourning your presence
in my quiescence.
Your essence I missed
of our last kiss.

A fragrance gently drifted in the air
I smelled your hair
I reached over in despair
I felt you weren't there.
I then said a prayer.

My bed still longs for you.
The sheets still mourn for you
They all ask for you.
What do I tell them?
.....I haven't a clue

Dreams blurred I can't accrue.
You're lips touching mine
It feels so true.
Benign, my mind's askew.

.......deeply craving you.

WHAT IS THIS HUMAN NEED…

What is this human need that I bare?
This emotional snare
We talk every day
Before I sleep and when I wake
I love you Lord
By my accord
And I know you're supposed to be everything to me
But within myself I feel hollow
As if something's lost
Nowhere to follow.

I miss her breath
I miss her smile
I miss her touch
And her curly red hair
Clinging on the shirts I'd ware
In Genesis you met Adams' needs
You said it wasn't good for man to be alone.
Why is it such for me?
Why must I bare this isolation?
My hearts bemoaned.

Why is it that:
My skin longs for touch
My ears long for her song
My nose longs for her breath
My lips for hers
Why Lord, why?

Have I fallen out of favor?
Am I now cursed and doomed?
Must I endure?

To wander and roam this planet alone.

DEAR BELOVED

Dear beloved,
I pray that the future man in your life
would recognize your true worth
As a treasure unearthed.

When he pursues you to be his wife
He'd handle you like
a delicate piece of fine China,
discovered at an antique store in Carolina.

He'd know your true value
Is like a rare gem stone, so true
gotten beneath the forgotten earth renewed,
which needs no honing with a such a succulent hue.

That your smile is beautiful
as the snowcapped mountains
And your loving youthful heart
waters the weary like an artesian fountain.

He'd know that your strength is not determined
by how much weight you can lift,
but how well you keep your family together
and yourself spiritually fit.

He'd know that words cannot ever
pierce your skin or break your heart.
because you are favored and covered
in the armor of God.
That which can never be taken away nor torn apart.

I LOVE YOU

I

… am alone without you.
A ship wrecked sailor,
on a leaky Boston Whaler.
Adrift on the Bearing Sea,
beyond my apogee.

Love

...is a cheap and an understated word,
when expressing how I feel about you.
If Love were a stone sized meteor,
the universe wouldn't have capacity enough
to contain it as you get nearer.

You

… are the only one the completes my soul
to make me feel whole.
When our souls unit as one,
they become the fiery light.
In an active galactic nuclei.

I'VE TRAVELED

I've traveled colds and weary flights
Frozen by the moonless nights
Through the echoes of silence
My heart's cadence continues
As my mind wonders away
To a distant place
Lost by the whispers of doubt
Trying to figure life out
Through this lonely path
To your grace
Where the masses met
To seek your face
This lifestyle of loneliness
Had worn me down
I was praying for death
To come around
But over the valleys I did see
Your light and its warmth
For My soul to keep
From this solitude
That seems to creep
Through the peace
And infinite love that I seek

SO, YOU SAY I'M TOO OLD

So you say I'm too old
And sooner than you
I'll reach my years of gold
What's a girl to do?

We're thirteen years apart
But I'm the only guy
That managed to tame your heart
And excite all of your parts!
You've loved other men
Near to your age
Who kinda put you in a cage
And got you feeling kind of queer
Like a hostage
Full of fear

Not me baby
My experience tamed your crazy
I've let you free to be yourself
Never putting you on a shelf
In my bed you squirmed and cheered
For the love I made with you
Was so dear
It took you to heaven
Places far and near
Heights never achieved
With any human nor machine
You Say my loving is great

And you've never experienced
Kindness as such
But because you discard
My loving for others
You'll have to get a crutch
Know you how much value
You've held in your hand
You've traded a diamond in the rough
For something made of sand
A cubic Zirconia
Or toy from Ionia
Like a child who would squalor
A shinny penny for a dollar

My loving makes your body tingle

And intermingled with your mind
Didn't my touch and kisses
Take you to places of pleasure
You never knew such bliss
I know it will be tough for you to find
Another love like mine.
Who'd whet your appetite
Of pure delight
Good luck at sorting through the rest
Now that you've discarded the best.

Adios mama!

DON'T BELIEVE THEIR LIES

Why is it that they're trying to divide us
Post black against white
Yellow against brown
Blondes against redheads
Brunettes against both
Brown eyes Against Green
Hazel eye against blue
What is it with this modern culture?
Do they not all know that we all started as one?
Do they not know that a woman's curves are beautiful?
Regardless of her color
There's certain qualities to dark skin
That light skin will never show
And a beauty to white skin
That dark skin cannot impersonate
And everything in between!
Beauty is in all colors.
Just choose your liking
Red, yellow or green skittles?

Why is it that they try to create a barrier between our languages?
A hillbilly is nothing but a "Hibaro"
That can speak English.
Whether it's from the jungles of El Younque,
The plains of Africa
Or the swamps of Florida
We all love nature
But have a distaste for hatred

There is no difference between the people in San Francisco
and San Juan
Mayaguez and Brooklyn
PRU or NYU
Australia or Ethiopia
We all bleed red
Have hearts that love
Don't let the imitators and impersonators fool you
They're all impostors
Who envy us
When we're united
As one people and one front

There isn't a wool big enough
To pull over all of our eyes.
So don't believe their lies.
For the Red White and Blue
Is made of many hues.

IN A PERFECT WORLD

In a perfect world
Nothing is as it seems
The bad guys bray
As the good guy
Gets locked away
The hero loses his job
While the zero gets promoted
And his incompetence Sugar coated

This Perfect world
Is a perfect illusion
A list of endless conclusions
Rich in theory poor in practice
Leery inclusions
With weary delusions
Protrude this perfect world view
To make the untrue Seem true

So forward I go
Unmasking the false prophets
That profit from perfection
And preach painless afflictions
Of smooth skin and tucked tummies
Skin colored like honey
With banished bruised blemishes
For money

For I know this to be true

CHAPTER TEN

For their arrived a perfect Jew
Whose prophetic presence
Was predicted and personified
To be justified as the perfect sacrifice
Whose cross denied deaths blow
and the sting of sin.
To him I sing!

No matter what condition I'm in…..
Jesus the King of kings.

I KNOW HOW TO WIN

I know how to win
And I know how to loose
Of which neither is a sin
Especially when I'm losing you
But another will come in your place
And replace the missing pieces of my heart

This I guarantee
Just like the guy that's with you
To which he too will loose
To the crazy games you play
The deceitful lies you say
And the dark path you choose

Ring in hand
Hope in his heart
If he doesn't sing and dance
To your tune
I know you'll tear him apart
Poor sucker I hope he's strong

To live through the misery
When you do him wrong.

YOUR BEAUTY IS DEEPER

Your beauty is deeper
Then what the eye beholds
As sweet as thy song is,
Sevenfold

Thy heart exuberates
Our ever loving Christ.
For your love for him,
There is no price.

For his love is ever lasting
Inside thy heart.
For your timeless inner beauty
Is what sets ye apart

With your hands by your side
Your palms facing up
I swore the angles cried
To Your grace is enough.

For I can only imagine
The feeling of your satin voice
That soothes their precious little hearts
That led them to rejoice.

For he is an everlasting God
Thy hearts so sincere
While keeping tempo apace

Oh when I see your tears!

As they roll down your face
Your hearts leaks His love
Like a broken vase
I can never get enough

As you sing Amazing Grace
It is well in my soul
For your voice is laced
With Gods wonders you behold.

For if I should fall
With your song I would know
That Jesus paid it all.
Many many years ago.

(Inspired by Britney and worship at HSC).

I CRAVE YOUR TOUCH

I crave your touch
Your smile
The way you devour me
With your eyes
And seeing your eyes
Turn from gray to blue...
Because I soothe you
I crave your body next to mines
And the feel of your heat on my thigh
I crave the pretty words you speak
As you kiss me on the cheek
The way you nibble my ear lobes
As you slowly disrobe
I crave your kisses to my chest
And the way you touch me
With your breast.
The scent of your breath
As you whisper sweet thing to my ears
With your Euro accent so clear
But most of all I crave us together
Because we've dreamt of each other.....

Forever.

WHERE'S THE LOVE IN THEIR VIOLENCE?

An innocent man is killed
For the wrong reason
It doesn't matter the season
Let's break out in riots
A black cop is shot in the street
No one cares
A white girl is beaten for her wallet
Left to die in a ditch
Dude reaches for his gun on a traffic stop
Is shot, and the world loses their mind
Violence breaks out, of all kinds

In their darkened hearts:
There's no love in their violence
There's no love in their riots
There's no love in their silence
There's no logic in their science

There's no love or peace in their words
Just the sound of tears,
The world has never heard
The pain still lingers
Like splinters of broken glass
The smell of burning flesh
Heaped in a pile of ash
Neither side is justified
In what they did
Not in the streets,

Nor their crib.

The love is lost
With all lives gone
Upon the night daylight seeps
The litter of rioters scattered
Throughout the streets
Smell of smoke and burning gas
In my clothes they seep
Death is forever!
But the things you stole
Are temporary
There's no love in their peace

My heart grows wary
Red skies in the morning
I'll take warning
Where are the profiteers of peace?
And the peddlers of propaganda?

Violence litters the Promised Land
And skewers the peace agenda
The lust of looting
Is in the rioters wreckage
The vestige of smoke and soot

Personified by their empty suites and boots.
Where's the Love their violence?

FORGIVENESS

What?
Forgiveness?
Areata are you nuts?
Did you just throw me under the bus?
Why should I have to ask her for it again?
I can't see it.
I didn't do anything wrong
She's the crazy one
Psyco persona like a crazy song!
She pulled me into this mess
Of continuous stress
To her I was just a meal ticket
With good smile
Who hung around for awhile
To raise kids till they were gone
Two daughters and one son
I raised them with all my best
Under the stress
That I was under
Hanging on
To everyone's wonder
Family, friends, acquaintances
Of present and past
Didn't know how long I'd last
They told me so, after the fact
How they'd see the things, we lacked
Love, unity, respect for each other
In front of them she'd say
"I only love him like a brother".

But swallow my pride, I will
This thing is harder to swallow
Then a golf ball sized pill
I'll ask her for it
To ease her pain
So that hurting monster
Will cease to hurt,

And release her chains.

CONCLUSION

S o there it is.
I failed over and over again, relationship after relationship, hoping to get better results, only to receive the same thing (the definition of insanity).

The thing that saved me was that I finally listened to God and did my best to learn from my mistakes.

A good friend of mine who is an expert horseman and one of my mentors once told me, "Val, you should never learn anything new, from the second kick of a horse. If by chance you ever get kicked again, take a note pad and pen and write down step by step what you did until you find out where you went wrong... By the way, do it away from the horse!"

And so I did. I haven't been in a relationship with anyone for a while now. And I don't intend to, until the time is right. I've reviewed and deeply thought about the poems, emails and conversations I've had with my lady friends and I am doing my best to better myself through reading books, listening to motivational and self-help CD's and pod casts, going to church and associating with friends with the same interests. From this moment forward I'll try to evaluate what productive, proactive things I've done for the week, so that I may readjust my heading. But most of all, I try to remember how many good memories I've made with people during my time with them. I've turned my mistakes into learning experiences. Every day I'm learning how to improve myself and the relationships I've made with people around me and afar.

I remember listening to a sermon at a "No Regrets" conference at Hope church. The speaker was talking about the Alter and the Ark of the Covenant. How, as you got closer to the Ark, the less and less people there are in its proximity. And how finally, only one person was allowed into the room with the Ark in it. And during that sermon I remembered how I gave access to my Heart (my Ark) to anyone and I came to the realization that I had to limit my access to it. Like the outer court, where many can be, were my acquaintances. In the tent were close friends. Inside the inner circle (where there were few) are my close relatives, and true friends who number about 3-4 people. The inside, where the Ark to my heart is, will only have space for that one special person. And that person will be vetted, and sanctified before being allowed full access.

What I've also learned, was that I had to be happy with me. I had to look the guy in the mirror and accept who he was and where he was in life, and be OK with him. And in doing that, I broke the codependency I had with women. I came to a realization that it's not who's by your side (arm candy, friends, family) that matters. It's about whose side you are on? God's side, is the only side to be on. The others are losing sides. I had to stop doing relationships poorly, as a relationship addict, and get my relationship with God onto better ground. I had to focus on building my relationship with Him instead of a person who was human and would eventually let me down. And if we are both pursuing a relationship with God, we would both be on the winning side.

I've also noticed and have come to the realization, that there is nothing greater than a man who walks and talks with God. I've seen it with some of the men I've hung around with. During the time of my depression I've strived to get back my "Godly strut". That "come at me bro" feeling of confidence, that you know you're on the winning side. His Side.

One day in a Singles Sunday School at Hope, this lady got up and gave her testimony. And in her testimony she spoke about how she had been mistreated as a child. And because of that, every relationship she had gotten into, was one where she was looking for affirmation that she was a good person and that somebody wanted her and loved her. She became the ultimate pleaser. And I related to her. I stood in a lousy marriage because I wanted to please my ex-wife, and my kids. I didn't care about myself, so I stayed in misery. And that wasn't their fault, it was mine. I own that, because I knew it was toxic from the get-go, and I, me, moi, decided to stay in it and try to fix it to please them and keep some sense of continuity for the kids. And in doing so, carrying this burden, I had lost my strut and myself.

Eventually, I learned that I had to put my pride aside and walk away from a bad marriage and own up that I had failed and learn how to live with it and move on to get my Godly strut back. But that was the problem here. How do I move on?

Back to my story:

After she gave her testimony at church, on the drive home I went into deep thought. I was struggling with my past and it was weighing me down. So I called the girl that gave her testimony in desperation. I wanted to know exactly what her secret was. How did she get rid of her past, and moved forward, to erase what had happened to her, and to live a happy and satisfying life.

How did she do it?

Every time I saw her she looked so happy and content.

How was that so, after going through what she did?

Her answer was staggering.

She told me, "Val you don't get rid of the pain of the past.

You learn how to live with it every day. Day by day. It never goes away. It's a constant and consistent struggle. And I've learned how to live with it and be happy with myself, by myself".

What?!? She struggles every day? Like me? Again my paradigm broke. And my thinking shifted.

I had to be happy with myself. No magic pill, monk chant or words would do it for me. It was an inside job. Stop focusing on the pain, and move forward, because the pain was going to be there anyway? Just like a runner going through "the wall" (that point of total exhaustion, when you're about to quit, but you press on even though your body is screaming at you to stop).

I had to live with my past mistakes, learn from them, and continue forward with complete disregard of the previous and present pain? The motion forward would release the pain that bound me. Hmm... I had to give that some thought for a while. It was a new way of thinking for me. I had always tried to analyze everything I've done (the engineer side of me), and tried to avoid previous and future mistakes. But this time, there wasn't any time to analyze, only time to move forward and continue. My previous experiences had now become part of me, like battle scars. Learn as you go, and move on. You don't learn anything new from the second kick of the horse. I had to stop trying to analyze my previous mistakes because it was causing me "analysis paralysis". You can't steer a parked car. And if the car stays in one spot long enough, it becomes a bombing range for pigeons. I'd linger too long thinking about my past and get depressed, and I'd fall back into my hole of depression.

Another thing that got me was that I had always thought that happiness was the destination. Just like when you finally buy a brand-new car, move into that bigger house, or get that Rolex you've always wanted. When I accomplish those things I realize that they were just that, "things". Don't get me wrong, there is nothing wrong with those things, and I'm a firm believer of rewarding yourself for accomplishments, but sometime we put more value on those things then we do on people, and our time, and that is where I faltered sometimes.

I came to the realization that I can make a million dollars, lose it, and within time, I can probably make it all back again. But if I lose one day of my life, it will never come back, I can never recover it. And that time was what I needed to place high on my value scale. Good relationships were what made me happy. I'm a very social and tribal guy. You are probably different then I am, so you need to figure out what is high on your scale. Personally, what makes YOU happy, and don't try to con yourself as to what it is either. So move on! Stop wasting time. Time stands still for no one.

I'd like to ask you this: What would you give to spent one day with a loved one that has already passed away?

In your dying days while in your hospital bed, are you going to be the person that says, "I should've spent more time in the office", or the person that said "I'm glad I spent more time ... (You fill in the blank).

Choose wisely my friends, "Time stands still for no one", and we only have one chance at this thing called "life". Enjoy the moments, and continue to realize that you control the "happy switch" inside of you.

The funny thing about success, be it big or small, is that the people that saw me achieve my goals, only saw the highlights, they never saw the struggle, the hardships, the relationships I had to dissolve, and the new relationships I had to grow, then incubate, and feed.

Happiness was in front of me all along. I was engaged in it and I didn't know it.

My happiness receptor switch was somehow turned off.

Undenounced to me, my happiness lingered in the memories produced with family, friends, coworkers, and good relationships. Moments when my friends and I swore we owned the night, moments of jubilee, sadness, victory and the coming together in defeat and death. The moments of helping a friend or stranger with no anticipation or expectation of having them pay it back. The gathering of amazing and incredible people and the journeys that we shared together. When I reflect back, that's what made me happy and continues to do so today.

Find out what flips your happy switch on, and pursue it. The pursuit will become your purpose. And the journey pursuing it will make you happy.

Valerio Henriquez is a network engineer for the Federal government of the United States, by trade, and has been on the cutting edge of technology. From living abroad on a nuclear submarine for months at a time while in the Navy, to becoming a major technical player for internet startup companies ("box with parts") during the internet boom of the 1990's.

All though he has a knack for technology, he's no regular techie. He's a New York raised Puerto Rican living in the marvelous Mid-South. He's also a writer, traveler, inventor, modern day thinker, an avid chess player, music lover of all genres', artist, and a submarine, motorcycle and car enthusiast. I hope you enjoy these select pieces of his story, poems, short stories and personal testimony. And let your imagination run wild with the images and thoughts they encroach.

If for any reason this book has helped you and you would like to contribute any positive feedback please feel free to email me at feedback@valeriohenriquez.com. I would love to hear your story.

Enjoy, and may God bless you all.

Valerio Henriquez

Submarines

Forever

Special thanks to:
Issac Curry, Memphis, TN. for his sermons and teachings.
www.Issaccurry.com

And the wonderful people at Hope Pres Church, Cordova TN.
www.hopepres.com

Thoughts, rants, and personal quotes

Sometimes a man is defined by the company he keeps while in solitude. - VH

Time rewinds for no man. -VH

When you surround yourself with losers you expect to lose and there's no way you can win.
When you surround yourself with winners you expect to win, and there's no way you can lose.
Success and failure begins with the people you surround yourself with.
Be very careful and choosy as to who you allow into your inner circle. -VH

I wasn't the architect of my own accomplishments.
Actually I was the saboteur of Gods plan for me. He kept trying to redirect me but I didn't listen
Thank you Lord for being persistent, and for your everlasting love. -VH

To the ladies of my past:
Thank you for the experiences we've shared. Because of that, you have made me love someone who I've never thought I'd ever love. Myself. - VH

I was cheering up a friend who had lost a limb in war. I was telling him how life had so much to give him now and so much to offer. And in cheering him and lifting him up. I realized that I too was gifted and had so much more to offer. My body parts were intact, my mind straight (with the exception of a few relationships), and my health and finances were fine.

A cheerful heart is like perfume in a spray bottle. When you spray it, droplets spray all around you, and they make the entire place so much better. I was blessed back tenfold by him. - VH

There are no happy endings. Because in the end we all die.

I think we've been brainwashed since we were children to find a happy ending.

We let this become our manifest destiny, and it consumes us to "BE HAPPY".

Well my friends I hate to break this to you, the truth is that we become so engulfed in the pursuit for a happy ending, that we disregard and forget the happy present that is in front of us. Happiness isn't a destination, it is a journey. Hence why the American founding fathers wrote that every man has the right to pursue happiness.

For example, when you go fishing, you prepare the line and bait, and you cast it into the water. Is it the preparation, the casting into the water or the waiting that makes you happy? No! It's when the fish is on the other side of the line, the fight, the capture, that admiration of the catch that engulfs you in excitement, then happiness. After wards the fish is put into the bucket with the others, and you continue fishing. Just like you pursuing the fish and its capture excited you and made you happy, so is life.

Pursue it and capture the moments! - VH

www.ingramcontent.com/pod-product-compliance
Lightning Source LLC
Chambersburg PA
CBHW060250100426
42742CB00011B/1701